Pretty Woman
Redeemed by Promise, Destined for Purpose
Joanne M. Green

ISBN: 978-1717325525

This book is available at quantity discounts for bulk
purchase. Please contact Joanne M. Green at the
following website:
www.ezraministriesinc.org

Scripture used in this book are noted From the *New King James
Version of the Bible* and the *Complete Jewish Bible*

Dedication

There are some amazing women in my life starting with my mother Lillian, sister Jacquelyn and special covenant friends Cynthia, JoLinda, Rosie and Veda. I not only dedicate this book to them but also to my spiritual sisters Cathy, Connie, Diana, Janese, Lisa, Maxine, Onia, Rhonda, Rosa, Sake and Susan and my spiritual daughters Nicole, Rachel and Vivian.

This book is also dedicated to my covenant friend Bishop Dorothy Washington and mentor Bishop Ernestine C. Reems.

Thank you all for your unconditional love, unwavering support, and pensive inspiration.

A very special "thank you "to Apostle Jerome and Pastor Betty Nelson for giving me the courage to fly, and to Madge for helping to make this project a reality!

Acknowledgements

Pretty Woman is an amazing work by new author Joanne Green. In this first work, Ms. Green has exhibited the force of a seasoned writer. She has skillfully woven together her captivating testimony of personal spiritual growth with simple yet profound biblical teaching. I recommend this book to anyone who enjoys an engaging personal story blended well with inspiring, practical truths. *Jo L. Harris, Author and Bible Teacher, Plano, TX*

Joanne Green has the unique ability to bring the word of God to life by using words in such a way that allows the reader to visualize the story from their own personal perspective. She inspires readers to connect the story to their private issues and find the cure in the word of God. She is a modern day "Anointed Prophet "used by God to facilitate healing of complicated generational family issues. ***"Pretty Woman"*** is a story that all can read over and over again that allows God to heal those hidden hurts in their lives. I encourage you to thrive, survive, and move forward as you read. *Pastor Connie Mc Grue, Prayer Warriors 4Life, Antioch, CA*

Joanne has an incredible way of blending biblical truths into immediate application that offers personal and spiritual value. Her ability to articulate her message eliminates false narratives that women tend to possess while recreating this wonderful picture of who we are in Christ Jesus. I appreciate her authenticity, transparency and personal life stories through *"Pretty Woman."* This book is going to transcend how women think of themselves. I trust you will open your heart and mindset to embrace that we are truly created in the image of God, fearfully and wonderfully made. *Cathy Moffitt, President, Heartfelt International Ministries, Inc., Arlington, TX*

Joanne Green is an anointed Woman of God that is extremely gifted in preaching and teaching the Word of God, as well as flowing in accuracy in the spiritual gift of the Word of Knowledge. She is a woman of integrity and adequately represents her ministry called Ezra Ministries. I am certain her new book *"Pretty Woman"* will be a best seller because her story will resonate with the heart of readers. *Apostle Jerome Nelson, Sr., Spirit of Life Ministries, Houston, TX*

Joanne is a gifted and anointed teacher with a beautiful way of speaking into all of our lives in this wonderful book called *"Pretty Woman."* Her message has a rich depth of revelation, wisdom, knowledge, and understanding of personal inner and emotional struggles to which all women from various cultural or ethnic backgrounds or life experiences will glean. She has powerfully and masterfully exposed Satan's strategy to destroy the hopes of those who have been truly *redeemed by God's promise and destined for purpose*. *Bishop Ernestine Cleveland Reems, Dublin, CA*

The atmosphere changes when Joanne walks in a room. Behind her smile, you would never know her story of heartbreak and tears. She is a woman of fervent effectual prayer with profound insight and solutions to everyday issues. Joanne's book, *"Pretty Woman"* will make you smile, bring you to tears, and give you Hope and inspiration despite your situation. *Bishop Dorothy W. Washington, Houston, TX*

Table of Contents

Introduction

I was led to revisit an old movie titled *"Pretty Woman."*
Watching the movie gave me a profound perspective I did
not have before. The Lord showed me aspects of the movie
that related to circumstances and mindsets in the lives of the
man and woman portrayed in the two main characters.

Mr. Edward Lewis is depicted as an astute billionaire
who is very successful in business, but very unsuccessful in
relationships. He is very absorbed in his business acquisitions
of purchasing struggling companies. He admits he had spent
little time nurturing his relationships, which cost him a
divorce and a breakup from a woman we hear complaining of
his neglect.

When Edward acquires these struggling companies,
they are purchased for far less than they are worth. He then
dismantles and destroys the lives that are attached to their
greatness. He has absolutely no interest in rebuilding them
but oh, how much pleasure and satisfaction he feels in
bringing them down. This is so typical of how Satan operates.
He is a thief and his job is to steal, to kill and destroy. He
takes great pleasure and satisfaction preying upon individuals
like you and me who have found themselves in vulnerable

1

positions. It is at those moments, and in those times, he tries to bring us down.

God on the other hand, is a master builder and chief architect of our lives who has gone to great lengths to rebuild and restore what has been broken and torn down by Satan.

When beckoned by his Spirit, we are lovingly brought to truths that will edify and build us up. ***Ephesians 4:16 says "the whole body should be joined and knitted together by what every joint supplies, according to the effective working by which every part does its share to cause growth of the body for the edifying of itself in love.*** By being interdependent on one another, our goal should be to encourage each other whenever the need arises. There is a nutritional spiritual supply that is received from those we are connected to within the body as well as those who may be connected just to our life's journey. When we receive what we need we are better positioned to accomplish our life's purpose because we have chosen to stay connected despite any difficulties that might arise. Think about it like this, when we sustain a cut to our finger, we do not cut it off just because it is injured. We allow the underworking's of the body to bring aid to the wounded or injured part. It might take several days, but ultimately the wound will mend and heal. The body works together to bring aid to the injury.

Vivian, the prostitute in this movie is a high school dropout with no hope of an aspiring future. She had been struggling to find suitable and respectable work. She ends up in Hollywood, where dreams are supposed to come true. In her search for any kind of work, she meets a prostitute whom she befriends. Her new friend gives her a place to stay and convinces Vivian that becoming a prostitute is not "so bad." I thought about how often Satan tells us that our sins are "not so bad," regardless of what kind of sin in which we have yielded. It could be an extra marital affair; fornication; alcohol or drug addictions or anything that has become a stronghold in our lives. We justify our behavior and keep living the fantasy. Others with whom there is a benefit reinforce the lie to make us feel better about our decisions. In the Father's eyes, sin is sin and He wants to not only remove the sin but blot the sin out of our history. The Bible says in the book of Isaiah, *"I have blotted out, like a thick cloud, your transgressions and like a cloud, your sins, return to me for I have redeemed you."* Wow; what a promise of forgiveness!

Vivian falls prey to the lie of Satan. She is all in and *the hooker has been hooked*, as she is later referred to in the movie. Satan will make sure you are not only labeled but that you are never free from whom others call you or who they perceive you to be. By managing her own business without the help of a pimp, she is in control of her own destiny. No matter how we look at our sin, Satan will always be the pimp behind our behavior and our sin becomes his badge to boast in his kingdom of darkness. Vivian further established a checklist and guidelines to justify her actions:

1. She would have her clients use condoms
2. She would visit the clinic monthly to stay safe from sexually transmitted disease
3. She would never kiss on the mouth
4. Oh yes, she would floss her teeth regularly and after every meal!

The problem with her decisions is that she is operating in deception while justifying her behavior. The greater impact of her decisions is that Vivian fails to realize she is worth so much more than she is selling herself. When we yield to low self-esteem, we do not acknowledge our self-worth or the value God has placed on our lives. We must not allow Satan to define us while intimidating us to embrace a false reality or narrative of our present life or circumstance. One of his strategies is to make sure we are intimidated with someone else's gifting, talents or abilities. Satan looks for these portals or entryways for him to steal, kill, and destroy our lives. First Peter 5:8 reminds us to be *"sober, be vigilant because our adversary the devil walks about like a roaring lion to seek whom he may devour.* Satan wants to gain access, do not give him any place in your life!

Throughout the movie, I saw many aspects that relate to our relationship with the Lord. This book is not about us being

> *When we do not value or respect ourselves for who God created us to be, we disrespect Him for who He is - Our Creator; Our Lover; Our Redeemer and Our Savior.*

"prostitutes, harlots, or hookers," but it is about behaviors that depict the mindset of prostitutes. In this section, I will explain how the *spirit of prostitution* tries to dominate our thinking and actions. I want to uncover attributes in our lives that depict the spirit of harlotry and prostitution that God said the children of Israel were guilty of, and how we can overcome those behaviors in our own lives. This is a spiritual implication and not necessarily a physical one. We can have victory in these places that cause us to abandon our relationship with the Lord because we feel guilty and downtrodden. A relationship that the Lord desires to have with us needs cultivating. This relationship has always been about His unconditional and unfailing love toward us. When we do not value or respect ourselves for who God created us to be, we disrespect Him for who He is - Our Creator; Our Lover; Our Redeemer and Our Savior. God has given us a unique imprint in our DNA; an imprint in our genetic coding that resembles what He created us to become. He fashioned our appearance as His expression of who we are to Him. We were created in His image and in His likeness to give Him pleasure. Colossians 1:16.

I heard God ask me this question:

- Do you respect yourself enough to change?
- Change the way you think.
- Change your mindset about some things in your life.
- Change your paradigms (your strong belief of a false principle – a religious dogma).

Now, I will ask you:

- Do you respect yourself enough to change?
- Change the way you think.
- Change your mindset about some things in your life.
- Change your paradigms (your strong belief of a false principle – a religious dogma).
- Are you ready to let go of some of those mindsets, religious doctrines, and false paradigms?

Pretty Woman is all about changing. It is about changing your perception of who you are and what purpose you have been created to fulfill. My hope is you will see the value of your past making an investment in your wonderful future. God's imprint in your life is sure to catapult you to a place far greater than you have ever imagined for yourself. His Kingdom is where "dreams are not only visualized, but they are brought to fruition." He has spoken your end from the beginning and God will complete His work in you.

Start the Transformation!

Pretty Woman

her lover named Harry.) Initially, in the movie she was actually a very attractive, normal sized woman. They were a "normal looking couple" and very much in love. Then something happened to her and she began to grow until she was 50 feet tall. Harry wanted nothing to do with her at that point and that is when his nightmare began. I could relate to this woman because she felt and looked like a freak and I felt and thought I looked like a freak.

> *When we see something and we embrace it, it goes into our soul and it becomes deeply rooted and embedded, and out of that root grows attributes that we have to deal with*

This woman's struggle was my struggle in relationships. I was so much taller than everyone in my world, and in my mind, it was the reason that made it difficult for boys to like me. At ten years-old I had already grown to be five feet, eight inches, and I was taller than my teachers, my classmates, and friends. I was somewhat of a phenomenon based upon the stares I would receive when in public. I remember being called the Jolly Green Giant in a grocery store by a small child who was terrified by my height. I need you to pay attention to this statement. When we see something and we embrace it, it goes into our soul and it becomes deeply rooted and embedded, and out of that root grows attributes that we have to deal with. Sometimes we are not equipped to deal with what we see about ourselves and need to seek counsel on the best path to our deliverance and healing. Therefore, in my world I was a standout in a negative way. Going to the movies or anywhere where an admission ticket was required, I would be required to pay the adult price unless I could prove my age. This was a wound in my soul. When I went trick or treating with my friends on Halloween, some of the adults would say, "You should be ashamed of yourself pretending to be a child to get candy." Some of the people would refuse to put candy in my Halloween sack. This was another wound in my soul. Not only was I tall; I was awkward and very clumsy. I was always told to be careful with that dish or watch where I was going because it was without a doubt I was going to break something or walk into something. Another wound planted in my soul.

I had other characteristics that I hated. My hair was unruly because it was short, thick, and frizzy. My mom had to hot press and laden it with grease to slick it down. My hair would then be braided to keep it tamed. I looked and felt like an un-kept child. Most of the girls I grew up with had features about them that I coveted. They were light skinned; some had long, pretty hair, some of them were on the petite size or average in size. Most importantly to me, they had the attention of the most popular boys in our neighborhood. They were also well liked by our peers and always a part of the in-crowd. Dating was out of the question for me because most of the boys were shorter, and they could not embrace my awkwardness. In fact, I went to my senior and college proms with my sister's boyfriend because I could not find dates. Again, this was another wound to my soul. I just so desperately wanted to be someone else instead of me!

I knew I should have been grateful to inherit my father's height who stood about six feet three inches and very handsome. However, in my child-sized mind, I knew that I had been cursed and dealt a bad hand. To make things even more complex, at my age and my height; my clothes did not fit properly. The sleeves on jackets and blouses were too short, and my pants looked like high water pants, which were not fashionable back then. Today, shorter pants are called Capris and are very fashionable. Shopping was always a big disappointment and let me not mention trying to find shoes that would fit my size ten feet. It was nearly impossible! The shoes in my size were so unattractive; I would try to squeeze my feet into the much prettier smaller shoe sizes. I convinced myself I also could walk in smaller shoes despite the pain I felt. I heard that Chinese woman would bind up their feet so they would remain small. I thought by wearing shoes that were too small, my feet would stop growing. How ridiculous was my thinking! First, wearing smaller shoes did not work. Second, I quickly developed corns and calluses on my toes that eventually had to be removed in my adult life.

Because I felt unloved, ugly, and unattractive, I became involved in promiscuous relationships. I was engaged to a man who unbeknownst to me smoked weed and could disguise his high times. I wound up having a child with him out of wedlock. I got to a point where his being high did not matter to me because he loved me. He was very handsome and reminded me of Omar Sharif and Billy Dee all wrapped up into one." I know some of you might not know who I am referring to, but trust me, he was very good looking. He had hazel eyes, a thick trimmed mustache; thick, curly black hair on light caramel skin. Initially, it did not bother me that he was two inches shorter than I was. At that time in my life, I just wanted someone to love me because I was pretty and he wanted to be with me. I did not care who he was, whether he was married, single, Black, White or hippie. I remember dating a Harvard college student who was a hippie. He loved my black skin and afro hairstyle. It got to a point where it did not matter who I was dating. When I found myself in the arms of someone who said that they cared for me, I found it easy for us to make love. I believed that silently he was saying, Joanne, I love you. For me to experience being loved in this manner allowed me to continue in my fantasies. I kept imagining it would be for forever, but it never was. This was how wrong and perverted my thinking had become.

I know for some of you; the hunt for real or imagined love has taken you to places in your life you regret or wish you never experienced. I know the pain of that deep-rooted rejection, the abandonment, and unfulfilled longing to be loved. Some of us, as adults have these same issues of abandonment and rejection. We feel ugly, all of these things are implemented by a spirit world that is real and tangible if we begin to discern with a discerning eye and a discerning ear. Whatever the flaw or issue is, Satan will keep it front and center in your life and he will try to build a stronghold of self-rejection.

I bring this up because today our society has made billions of dollars defining what pretty looks like. Advertising companies have defined us by advertising products to make us pretty, prettier, and the prettiest. Many of us have bought this lie, so we have spent too much money on buying the right hairstyle, the right kind of clothes, handbags, and shoes. Not to mention we purchase weight reduction products, we undergo cosmetic surgeries; liposuction and breast augmentation enhancements, while others, are prisoners of sinful lifestyles and secret addictions. We have secrets about ourselves that we keep covered up and those secrets have kept us in bondage. We all have places in our past that seem distant to our present state.

Within your environment called SELF and the realm of influence called YOU! You are in for an extreme makeover; there is no charge! You are paid in full by God.

Watching *"Pretty Woman"* helped me to identify behaviors, and extract some profound insights and realities about outward character and inward pain that deeply flaw our humanity. It is my hope with this book that you'll be ignited and inspired to dig deep within yourself to find the treasure and the jewel you are to our Father. All of us are a treasure fashioned by God. With his creative hand, you are to be formed to His image of beauty and holiness. Within your environment called SELF and the realm of influence called YOU! You are in for an extreme makeover; there is no charge! You are paid in full by God.

When you look up the definition of **pretty**, it is defined as pleasing or attractive to the eye." However, the origin of the word is defined as cunning, skillful, and artful. We have heard this word before. Satan was "cunning and skillful and artful" in the way he seduced Eve in the Garden of Eden. Look up the scriptures in Genesis chapter three. Well, by the 1400s cunning was redefined as manly and gallant. By 1440, the definition changed from attractive to, skillfully made to fine, and then defined as "beautiful." It is interesting to me in the Bible, "pretty" is mentioned only one time in the New King James Version. Jeremiah 46:20 states; *"Egypt is a very pretty heifer, but destruction comes, it comes from the north."* Jeremiah 1:14 *says, "Out of the north calamity shall break forth on all the inhabitants of the land."*

Let us look at this one word at a time:

If we look at the word **Egypt,** it is usually spoken of as a place of bondage for God's chosen and well-loved children. The children of Israel had a hard taskmaster named Pharaoh. Life was hard for them in captivity. The Hebrew people were not free to be who God called them to be. God saw them as His chosen, his own special people. The

Hebrew people were designated by God as a royal priesthood who would inherit and become a royal nation. They were to inherit a land flowing with milk and honey, but instead they were in captivity making straw and building Pharaoh's city. Some of us are in captivity and Satan is using us to build his kingdom by our outward expressions of behavior and our inward pain that has been suppressed.

Pretty in this context is symbolic of operating from a cunning place. You know that Satan was pretty and he was cunning. Satan will always be a hard taskmaster when he catches you operating in his realm of dominion and power. When you are caught by Satan, you will be held as his hostage and will remain in captivity until you are set free by truth! Whatever we allow to soothe our pain of rejection, our need for acceptance or our need to feel loved; it will become a stronghold. It could be alcohol, drugs, lust for power, sex or any number of things that we have allowed to mask our excruciating never-ending pain.

In this study, we are going to examine the spirit of prostitution. God calls prostitution a spirit of harlotry.

Heifer is defined as an inexperienced, untrained female who produces nothing. This woman never gives birth to anything. A heifer woman is barren and unfruitful. Amos 4:1 describes for us metaphorically a heifer as a voluptuous female in Samaria. Hence, we get our slang words for "you old heifer". Heifer alludes to a high stepping female referencing a prostitute. I do not want anyone to become offended because I am going to talk about spirits that display themselves through outward manifestations of bad behavior that stems from inward pain.

To be clear I believe God would say to us, woman of God, downtrodden woman, abandoned woman, rejected woman, woman of color, or woman of insignificance, WOMAN you do not have to be slaves in bondage who belong to the pimps of the world!. You do not have to be cunning; manipulative; high stepping prostitutes who portray themselves as inexperienced; untrained and incapable of producing fruit or living fruitful, productive lives. WOMAN you are not barren as you suppose!

1

Note: Prostitutes sell their bodies, they are in the business of selling, or merchandising what is known as their goods or services. Spiritually speaking one could sell or merchandise their gifts; their talents or the anointing God has bestowed or given to individuals. In this study, we are going to examine the spirit of prostitution. God calls prostitution a spirit of harlotry.

The North Wind symbolically was a destructive wind, which destroyed everything in its path. Some of you have had North winds blowing profusely in everything you try to erect or build. Satan uses these headwinds to tear down everything meaningful in our lives. Some of you are met with calamity and turmoil constantly. In this teaching, you will learn to identify the spirits behind the activity and take dominion over Satan and cancel his assignment against you!

I hear some of you saying to yourself; "but I am not a prostitute." You might also say; "this certainly doesn't apply to me because I live a rather good clean life." (I mean I occasionally end up in a sexually centered relationship, but it is not as you say.) Well, I am glad you feel that way, but could it be that God wants to open up a realm in your life? From your past, is there a bruise or a wounded place that you have covered up because of the tendency to look outwardly instead of honestly looking inwardly? God wants to pour His healing

20

balm on some of those places and bring you to wholeness. Often times God deals with the layers and layers of truth about our trauma that need to be removed in order for us to know where we are with Him. He wants to take His anointing oil, the Balm of Gilead, to rub over the place prior to his surgery to tap into that wounded place. His own spiritual healing process will allow us to experience His healing power and virtue that He wants to dispense. This is necessary for growth and development as mature children of God. *We have to look at this from a spiritual aspect.*

God mentions harlots in the book of Genesis, Exodus, Leviticus, Deuteronomy, Joshua, Judges, the Chronicles, the Psalms, Proverbs, Isaiah, Jeremiah, Ezekiel, Hosea, Joel, Amos, Micah, Nahum, Corinthians, Hebrews, James, and Revelation. Harlots are mentioned in twenty-three of sixty-six books of the Bible. God deals openly with the spirit of harlotry so many times; because I believe, He wants to make a point of how not to become caught in the same entrapments.

Harlot is a term he uses to refer to His children rejecting Him as their lover. The word Harlotry is used symbolically to reference the lewd display of sexual and immoral behavior prevalent among His children. God is a very jealous lover. Have you ever had a jealous lover? Have

2

you ever tried to make someone jealous over you? Do you remember the extremes you went to, to get your lovers attention? There were times in my life and in my relationships that I felt I needed to seduce, manipulate and entrap someone into giving me the love I desperately wanted or needed. This was a false perception. Listen to me; God hates to be rejected. His covenant name is Jehovah Kanna. God made you unique and for His pleasure, and His pleasure alone. Look up the scripture, Colossians 1:16. One of our commandments was not to have any other gods before Him. God wants to be at the center of our love and affection and demonstrate His love towards you and me.

I believe there are times when we believe that He made a mistake with how we look or what course we have taken to remedy a flaw that was the imprint of his doing. We think it is a flaw in us but it is an imprint uniquely given to us for his distinction. David who had come to know himself as a flawed individual gives us deep and personal insight when he reminds us that the master craftsman, and Creator God, formed each of us inwardly, covering us in our mother's womb; made us skillfully, fearfully and wonderfully. Then, God called His work Marvelous! Did you hear that you are a *marvelous* work piece of God!

We must not allow Satan to rob us of intimate encounters with God our Lover. God loved us before we knew the real meaning of love. The Word says God loved us while we were yet in our sins. I am telling you, this is some kind of love. God is the one who causes us to grow and mature. He uses circumstances in our lives to mature us. He wants to position us in a right relationship with Him whereby we conceive and give birth to all that He has planned for our lives. He is a lover that understands our thoughts from afar. He understands our path and is acquainted with all of our ways. There is not a word on our tongue that God doesn't already know according to the scripture. Look up Psalm 139. God's desire for you and me is that we would not be barren or unfruitful according to 2 Peter 2, because we know and understand His divine nature and power. He has given us everything we need to live emotionally sound, physically endowed, and abundantly supplied Godly lives.

Pretty Woman

Chapter Two:

Spirit Activity

Since we do not wrestle against flesh and blood but against spirit activity, we are going to look at some specific spirits that harass us and make us feel certain ways. Some of us may already be well equipped in this area. I believe if we open ourselves to truth, and listen with a new set of ears, then you will gain a new tool for spiritual warfare. Jehovah Gibbor is the covenant name for the Lord is Mighty. The Lord is a Mighty Man of war. He teaches our hands to war, and our fingers to fight. By using His might and power in spiritual warfare, we will know how to identify the spirits that harass and intimidate us. We will become more successful in transforming the areas of our lives we feel are inadequate.

Three spirits have aligned themselves together to form a powerful, destructive force against us. I call them the spirits of J.A.D. (Jezebel, Athaliah, and Delilah). We will get more into each of these spirits later in the book. When we see the activity of these spirits, we will be able to identify and deal with the individuals more effectively and we will see lasting transformation. Our foundation will begin by looking at Hosea, chapters one and two.

Before we delve into these chapters, I was reminded to share with you a situation that occurred when I was very young. In Hosea, we will see that He calls his children Harlots. Remember, we are talking about a spirit that manifests through behavior. He uses the words harlot and prostitutes metaphorically to describe the behaviors that seem to be prevalent among His children.

If we think about what **Harlot** means, a good definition would be "one consecrated or devoted to prostitution in connection with abominable worship." Abominable worship is the worship of anything outside of the worship of God.

When we think about the *spirit of prostitution*, we are thinking about a base or unworthy use of a talent or ability. When we prostitute our gifts or our ability, and sell, merchandise or promote our gifts, we are referring to the spiritual sense of harlotry and prostitution. Notice in the book of Hosea, God describes perfectly the behavior of His people. God also sets a standard and a deliverer in the midst of the people. Before we go there, I want to share something very personal. I recently shared this at a women's conference where the Holy Spirit wanted to do something with the information I was releasing.

When I was thirteen or fourteen, I was feeling like a freak because I was awkward and clumsy. A door opened to my sexuality. Just like in the Garden of Eden, Adam and Eve did not know they were naked until they sinned. Following the sin, they departed from God through disobedience.

When I was between the ages thirteen and fifteen, a neighbor fondled me and showed me how to masturbate. I had forgotten that incident. This was an open door; an access point that the enemy used in my later years to cause me to make some decisions that I certainly regret. I had low self-esteem and because I was rejected by my peers and because I felt awkward, the enemy had an open portal and right to plant seed that would later erupt in my adult life. As a result, when I was divorced, the door opened wide because of a feeling of abandonment. I had been rejected and I was in great pain. My marriage had ended and the divorce was final right at my fortieth birthday. One evening, I remember feeling very alone, feeling very depressed and missing my relationship of marriage. The oppression that I felt was intense, so much so, that all of my sexuality was heightened and taunting. It was about 10:00 p.m. that night and I found myself putting on a pair of jeans and a denim shirt. I did not bother to put on any undergarments because I wanted quick and easy access. I needed to get rid of the pain. All I could think about was to get to the red light district as fast as I could to relieve myself of this drive for sex. I wanted to be held and embraced by someone, anyone who needed me. I was not in my right mind. I wanted to feel loved by someone, and anyone who needed me. This is how perverted and deranged our thoughts are when we do not bring our thoughts and emotions to the power and presence of God.

When I got to a place in the red light district where I could leave my car and walk a distance down the street, I remember walking up to a car and offering myself as a "free trick." The man rolled down his window when I approached it. I felt sure that I had scored a solicitor, but what happened next was unexplainable to me. After I finished speaking to him, he looked at me as if I were crazy, rolled up his window, and drove away. I did not understand what had happened. You would think that would have sent me home. Nope, I was on the hunt to get my pain soothed. I was being driven by a spirit outside of myself. I made my way down by the nearby lake and sat on the grass. I said to myself the first person that comes in my direction I would go for it. Well to my amazement, a young man came and sat beside me. He was grubby and was not very appealing; he just looked awful. I thought to myself that he must have been a homeless person. He started a conversation with me while I sat on the grass.

He asked "what are you doing out so late?" It is almost midnight, he said. I said, "I am just trying to get some air." He asked my name; well I knew not to give him my name, so I said what is your name? He told me his name and then I asked where he was from. He said Mississippi. I said, "Oh that's where some of my ex-family members were from." I asked him what part of Mississippi was he from and he told me exactly the same city where my ex-husbands' family grew up. I then said, "Well, who do you know there?" He said, "I have been in Dallas for a while, but I am going back to Mississippi because I have really good friends and a lot of family there. He said, "I know the Greens! I said; really, "who in that family do you know?" He then began to list my ex-husband and most of his fourteen sisters and brothers. It was as if God slapped me up side my head! I got up from there and said; "I have got to go." Today, as I think about that night, I believe that it was God's ministering Angel and the Grace of God that prevented me from making a disastrous decision that night. To say the least, I came to myself and quickly got in my car and drove home. I cried out to God uncontrollably with tears rolling down my face. I felt alone, abandoned and unloved. I cried, "God if you don't take these feelings away from me, and if you don't help me through this; I know I won't stay saved."

Why do I share this part of my painful past? There are times in our relationship with the Lord when we play the harlot. I was literally trying to become a harlot. We will find ourselves estranged from our relationship with God when we give the enemy an open door to temptation. He will ensnare us or entangle us by using these spirits of oppression, depression, abandonment, or rejection. This is why these spirits need to be dealt with at the root.

In the story of Hosea, God tells him to take Gomer as his wife. Hosea's name means salvation. In the Old Testament, when his name is being referenced, God is signifying deliverance for his people from evil and danger. When salvation is mentioned in the New Testament, God is saying that He wants deliverance from guilt and pollution or contamination of sin and that is why Jesus came to be the Redeemer of our sin and redemption for us. He tells Hosea to marry Gomer, whose name means vanishing (the wanderer). Gomer is a prostitute, wandering from one relationship to another. Salvation and wandering are brought together so that the salvation Hosea represents redeems Gomer from her wandering. This is the subject of the first two books of Hosea. I believe that this is very important because Hosea was the only prophet to document the written prophecy. He was very detailed about the spirit that plagued the children of Israel.

Hosea marries Gomer who continues to wander from one relationship to another. I know that some of us can relate to this, because we too have gone from one relationship to another; trying to fill the void that only, God is able to fulfill.

God opens Gomer's womb, signifying she will no longer be barren or unfruitful. She will give birth to three children; the firstborn Jezreel whose name means "God scatters;" her second born; Lo Ruhamah, whose name means, "not pitied," (God temporarily rejects his daughter), and the third child is Lo Ammi, whose name means "not my people," (God temporarily disowns His daughter). In the context of the scripture, the children of Israel were scattered, rejected, and temporarily disowned. These feelings should be real and tangible to us. The message in these scriptures is; a Savior was being sent to save a prostitute. We can glean from an underlying truth. God is making a profound statement to us, saying I am *married* to you and I want to be the *God of your Salvation, I am your Redeemer.* God is saying He will come to you when you feel rejected and when you feel disowned.

In our story, in chapter two of the book of Hosea, God wants Hosea to place a hedge around Gomer; so she will find it difficult to find and chase after lovers. The hedge would cause Gomer to stop fornicating. We are talking about spiritual fornication, so please do not be offended here, unless you are involved in a relationship where fornication is part of that relationship. Stop that activity. We need to take the time to identify behaviors in our relationship with the Lord that alienates us from His presence. Later in this book, we will talk about false worship through a religious spirit, through low self-esteem and through a host of other things. The children of Israel were constantly engaging in spiritual fornication and rebellion towards God. They were acting out, like spoiled and untrained children. They had become oppressed by the enemy because they gave the enemy access through their behavior.

Fornication is defined as being joined to something or someone, and there is an exchange made or a deposit is made and there is a birthing of the behavior, which was conceived. For example, when you join yourself to Satan through doubt, then fear is birthed. It is just like Adam and Eve, in the Garden of Eden. Eve entertained and embraced doubt and opened the door to fear. The fear exposed their nakedness to one another. At that moment, they were separated from God. God had to devise the plan of redemption to bring them back through reconciliation. This is the same situation here.

While we are talking about spiritual fornication, we must deal with physical fornication and sexual immorality. Hosea 2:6, 7 says; *therefore, behold, I will hedge up your way with thorns, and wall her in, so that she cannot find her paths. She will chase her lovers but not overtake them; yes she will seek them but not find them, then she will say I will go and return to my first husband.* Hosea is told to hedge-in Gomer to protect her. (God) wants Gomer to stop looking on the outside of her for what she thinks she needs. She must begin to look deep within to find her inner beauty, strength, and purpose. We too must find our strength and inner beauty and purpose. Hosea prays that she will return to him when she remembers that it was Hosea, her husband; who has what she needs, spiritually, physically and emotionally. Hosea covered her nakedness. God wants to cover your nakedness, those not so lovely places in your past and for some of you, your present situation. God covered my nakedness and me. God removed me from a destructive path that could have derailed and aborted His plan and purpose for my life. Ultimately, Gomer calls Hosea her husband and no longer is dominated, governed, or driven by a hard taskmaster. Hosea and Gomer will live in covenant. I had to call and cry out to God and see Him as my Husband and just like Gomer and Hosea, I would find myself joined together in holy matrimony with Jehovah Kanna, my lover. What a picture of God as our Lover, going to such great extremes to love us out of our pursuit of other things, and to win our hearts and restore our virtue.

I want us to know how attractive and beautiful we really are, apart from what we see in the mirror of man. Look in the mirror of God's Word to define how others will look upon you. They will see the favor of God surrounding you like a shield of protection according to the scripture, Psalm 5:12 *Let the Lord's countenance be upon you and give you peace,* according to Numbers 6:26. Remember, we are the apple of His eye according to Zechariah 2:8. Remind yourself daily that He has clothed you with garments of salvation and covered you with the robe of righteousness as stated in Isaiah 61:10; *Dance to the song of Zephaniah that says so greatly rejoice in your Lover O daughter and be joyful way down in your soul! Sing, O daughter of Zion, God is in your midst and He is dancing and rejoicing over you with gladness, he will quiet you with His Love.* Zephaniah 3:14-17. God's Agape Love, which is unconditional, will cloak us and cover us.

We are His precious *"Pretty Women"*. We have been fashioned in the image of an all-knowing God. He knows every weakness and every infirmity that plagues us. He knows the strategies that the enemy might use against us to try to separate us from His love. Yet He redeemed our life from destruction and crowned us with His tender mercies. He has become our Kinsman Redeemer and purchased all that was stolen through the disobedience of Adam and our disobedience. He has restored our right to become His bride. A bride adorned with splendor, majesty and beauty that is incomprehensible to those who have no covenant. As a bride readies herself for her wedding day, so prepare yourself for Him. Make sure your wedding dress is free from spots or wrinkles. Every one of us has a responsibility to identify our spots on our wedding dress. I am not talking about food stains or dirt; I am talking about low self- esteem, doubt, and fear, sexual immorality that we become involved in. I am talking about anger and deep-rooted bitterness, un-forgiveness, and resentment. There is trauma in our lives that needs to be reconciled and healed. I believe that God wants to uncover each layer and unveil those hidden bruises, wounds, and scars so we can see them in the way He sees them, and receive from *Him, His Healing Balm, His Restoration, and Reconciliation.*

God is loving and I am so glad that he revealed to me a door that had been opened when I was young. I was spiritually ignorant at that age and the roots were hidden for many years, but Satan knew how to retrieve it at just the right time to try to hinder and abort the plan of God for my life. This is what he is attempting to do in some of your lives right now. There could be issues in your lives that have not been dealt with and they are plaguing you today. Maybe they are generational or maybe they have just occurred. Maybe there are situations and circumstances that you cannot articulate or will not talk about when God tries to open the door for healing. Now is the time to deal with these issues and receive His healing and forgiveness. I could have dwelt on my past and thought about how atrocious my behavior had become; not realizing that when you are in pain, and traumatized; you just want the pain to go away. You find ways to mask the pain or soothe the pain or even put a temporary Band-Aid on the pain without really dealing with the pain. God knows about your pain and God wants to deal with your issues. He dealt with the children of Israel calling them harlots and He said that they were plagued with a spirit of prostitution. However, He lovingly brought them back to Himself with a plan of redemption. Let Him bring you back to that place of healing. Let God work in your life and thank Him for His Grace!

Just because we live in a dispensation of Grace does not give us the right or permission to continue our bad behavior. Paul says in Romans chapters six and seven that Grace is certainly available. Since Grace is available, why should we keep on sinning? At some point, we come to the realization there is no big sin or little sin. Sin removes us from our intimate place with God just as Adam and Eve were removed from an intimate place of God walking with them in the cool of the day. They all enjoyed each other's company and conversation. They had to literally be removed from the place He called His Garden of Eden. They could no longer enjoy His fellowship.

Anything that is not of faith is sin in the eyes of God. God expects us to walk by faith. Through faith, we use the tools He has given to us to identify the spirits that plague and torment us, remove the hindrances and put Satan under our feet. We must be honest and be willing to confess our sins, one to another: as the Lord leads us to seek out help or counsel. I believe in using wisdom as we share intimate places about our pasts, but I have to trust Him regarding the pathway of my healing and my deliverance. I am free to share my story, because I have been healed and totally exonerated, and cleansed by His blood. I know that my story will set someone else free, yours will too. Someone needs to hear your story. We are all working out our own soul salvation and deliverance. We all have something in our past; something we have kept secret; something that God wants to uncover so He can cover us with His grace and unconditional love. There is no shame in our game. I think that is why some have been turned off with Christianity, religion and the church because the church will not be real. Instead of compassion, some churches offer criticism and condemnation. As a minister of the gospel of Jesus Christ, I have felt an obligation to tell my story, and how I came through my situation. "YOU as a minister of reconciliation can come through too!"

Let others be witnesses to God's transformational power and workings in our lives. Let's provoke one another to passionately seek God as our Lover. Let us get to the roots of our issues. It is time to ready ourselves, and adorn ourselves as His Bride and prepare for His return.

When we look at the plight of our Nation, you only have to discern that the signs of the times are pointing to His coming, His soon return. If you listen closely, you will hear the *"Spirit and the Bride say, "Come!" and let him who hears say, "Come!" And let him who thirsts come. Whoever desires let him take the water of life freely, Revelation 22:17.*

The time has never been more urgent; do not delay; your Lover awaits you!

The Spirit of Harlotry

Remember, in the movie, Vivian, is the prostitute. Because she cannot get away from her past of being a high school dropout and looking at a future without respectable work she falls prey to Satan's lies. She cannot see how low self-esteem and no self-worth play into his narrative about her. She convinces herself that prostitution is not "so bad." Satan will always remind us that our sins are not so bad. He will point to our society of socially accepted behavior. Today our society of acceptance says it is:

- **alright** to have sex outside of marriage;
- **alright** to be in same sex relationships;
- **alright** to be involved in adulterous relationships;
- **alright** to take prescription meds to mask our pain and to help us sleep;
- **alright** to smoke crack, do drugs to put us in a state of euphoria to keep us from facing our true realities.

The list is never ending because we have *socially accepted* these behaviors. We have become numb to His Holy presence. These patterns of behaviors become strongholds in our lives that Satan makes sure are perpetuated. Vivian is held captive and she does not even realize that she is in a prison and Satan is her pimp and master.

An Exercise

The following is an exercise, which will help you to identify some behaviors that depict how the spirit of harlotry is manifested. It is important for you to recognize the strategies of the enemy that would keep you bound and allow his strongholds to entrap and ensnare you to your own detriment. Vertically I have written a letter starting with the letter **H** and then horizontally I have written an attribute or behavior that sometimes can be evident in us or in our relationships. Please note that this is not an exhaustive list.

As you will see, these patterns or these behaviors are hidden or rooted in the Spirit of Harlotry. They might operate in us or in others as ruling powers or principalities. They are strongholds that govern the behavior. The Bible tells us that we do not wrestle against flesh and blood, but against principalities, against powers, against rulers of darkness of this age and against *spiritual hosts of wickedness*. In other words spiritual activity manifested in outward behavior.

H   Hopeless; hurt; harassed; hateful; hassled; heartbroken; headstrong; hostile; humiliated,

A   Agitated; argumentative; abusive; addicted; angry; anxious; abandonment; ashamed; abortion,

R   Rude; rebellious; ridiculed; resentful; reckless; restless; rejection,

L   Lesbian tendency or behavior; loner; lost; liar; lonely; lustful; lewd,

O   Opinionated; outrageous; oppressed; offended; obnoxious; obsessive,

T   Threatened; troubled; taunted; terrified; traumatized; tormented; trapped,

I was able to see through my own life and lifestyle how Satan used hurt, loneliness and rejection to gain entrance into my life to derail and delay the plan of God for my life. You must realize that the spirit of harlotry is a ruling power that becomes a stronghold. If you can begin to identify these outward manifestations or attributes in your own life or in the life of others, you will not buy into the lie of Satan when he comes to seek and destroy your life or your life's purpose. You will also be able to help set the captives free.

God is often symbolically referencing his children as being beguiled by the *spirit of harlotry*. We also saw this same spirit oppressing and driving Gomer in her behavior in Hosea. In dealing with this subject, we must separate the person or persons from the spirit and confront the spirit activity. Jesus came to set the captive free, and by opening the prison doors, we must do the same. The Holy Spirit, our helper, our Paraclete, is the Spirit of Truth who can and will reveal demonic activity within us or within others. Not everything is a spirit. There are some behaviors that are manifested in behaviors based on choice and results in a consequence of the choices made.

Remember, Adam and Eve suffered a consequence of a choice they made to sin. They succumbed to the temptation of Satan. Adam and Eve had specific instructions and they chose to disobey those instructions. They gave Satan legal access and they opened the gate for him to become pimp and master. He then had the authority to operate in the earthly and heavenly realms as the ruler of darkness releasing his demons and demonic spirits into the earth. We can learn how to navigate the heavenly realm by praying powerful prayers that are formulated with the word of God to disarm Satan and putting a stop to his activity when we pray with the authority God has given us.

The Unclean Spirits

I want to be very clear and help us understand that "spirit activity" is real. Satan and his demons need a body to operate in the earth realm. I want to sidetrack for just a moment to help you visualize just how foolhardy and dangerous it is to give permission to Satan to overpower you in any area of your life.

In order for us to become more effective in defeating demonic activity in us and in others, we must understand that Satan is looking for your permission to gain access through your choices, through your circumstances or unfortunate situations.

First Peter 5:8 reads: *Be sober, be vigilant; because your adversary the devil walks about like a roaring lion, seeking whom he may devour. Satan is like a roaring lion seeking whom he may devour.*

Now read Job 1: 6-12. You will see that Satan is asking permission from God to have access to attack Job.

6 Now there was a day when the sons of God came to present themselves before the Lord, and Satan also came among them. 7 And the Lord said to Satan, "From where do you come?" So Satan answered the Lord and said, "From going to and fro on the earth, and from walking back and forth on it." 8 Then the Lord

43

said to Satan, "Have you considered my servant Job, that there is none like him on the earth, a blameless and upright man, one who fears God and shuns evil?"

Verses 11, 12: But now, stretch out your hand and touch all that he has, and he will surely curse You to Your face!" And the Lord said to Satan, "Behold, all that he has is in your power; only do not lay a hand on his person." Satan went out from the presence of the Lord.

> *There are times in our lives that God will allow Satan to test our faith just like Job but will set limitations in our testings and trials.*

Satan acknowledges that God had a hedge around Job and that he would need permission to attack him. There are times in our lives that God will allow Satan to test our faith just like Job but will set limitations in our testing's and in our trials. We must not knowingly give any place to Satan. Satan will seek to find open access points in your life to see if he has legal rights to attack, but let him find your doors and portals locked and bolted. These doors; access points or entryways could be behavior manifested as rejection, isolation; abandonment; fear, a lying spirit; pride etc. If Satan sees any manifestations of activity that belongs to his kingdom, he will automatically have a legal right to steal, to kill and to destroy. Let's look at Mark 5:1-12 *Then they came to the other side of the sea, to the country of the Gadarenes. And when He had come out of the boat, immediately there met Him out of the tombs a man with an unclean spirit, Who had his dwelling among the tombs; and no one could bind him, not even with chains, Because he had often been bound with shackles and chains. And the chains had been pulled apart by him, and the shackles broken in pieces; neither could anyone tame him. And always, night and day, he was in the mountains and in the tombs, crying out and cutting himself with stones. When he saw Jesus from afar, he ran and worshiped Him. And he cried out with a loud voice and said, "What have I to do with You, Jesus, Son of the Most High God? I implore You by God that You do not torment me."*

For He said to him, "Come out of the man, unclean spirit!" Then He asked him, "What is your name?" And he answered, saying, "My name is Legion; for we are many." Also he begged Him earnestly that He would not send them out of the country. Now a large herd of swine was feeding there near the mountains. So, all the demons begged Him, saying, Send us to the swine, that we may enter them. And at once Jesus gave them permission."

In this chapter, we are met with a man who was living among the tombs who is possessed and oppressed with an **"unclean spirit"**, or in other words, he was possessed by multiple spirits. He was living among the dead. Everything around him was void of life. In Verse 3, the Bible is clear to let us know that those who had come to him found it difficult to restrain him. In other words, all that had come were rendered powerless over this man because "no one could bind him" or "tame him". The word tame defined means to control. This man was out of control.

Upon further study, we come to realize that this spirit is not one spirit but many spirits and his name is Legion. The dictionary defines the word legion **as a very great number; a Roman army comprised of 3,000-6,000 soldiers or any large group of armed men.** To say the least, in the depiction of this man, it is clear he was possessed and being tormented by a great number of spirits. These spirits were very powerful; strong and kept him in their control and in captivity.

We also know from this passage of scripture that this man was under the influence of a **religious spirit** and he had *knowledge* of Jesus but did not have a **relationship** with Him. He addresses Jesus as the Son of the Most High God but wants nothing to do with Jesus the Savior or Deliverer. This spirit was mocking Jesus and had no intention of surrendering.

We should thank God, that there are times in our lives when the Savior and the Deliverer Jesus Christ just shows up to set us free from our captivity. Jesus does not allow the **unclean spirit** any room to keep this man bound any longer. He immediately commands that the spirit come out of the man. Notice Jesus makes a distinction between the man and the spirit. The authority of the Word Jesus is all that is needed to release Satan's prisoner.

In this ministry encounter, the disciples had **not yet** been given the power that was on display. They were mere eyewitnesses to that Power and Authority!

Today, as believers, we have not only been given the authority to use His name; but we are anointed and empowered by the Holy Spirit *"to proclaim liberty to the captive and to set at liberty those who are oppressed.*

Luke 4:18. We also have been given a key weapon found in Matthew 18:18, 19 which states, *"whatever we bind on earth will be bound in heaven and whatever we loose in earth will be loosed in heaven. If two of us agree on earth concerning anything that we ask, "It will be done for us by our Father in heaven.*

    Sometimes we are ineffective in waging warfare against Satan and demonic activity in this area because we do not fully understand the terminology or our legal authority against his kingdom. We must learn to identify the specific spirit and spirit activity that is on display or in manifestation when we encounter someone who is being held hostage by the enemy. This spirit had a name, its name was Legion, and he was host to other spirits of wickedness.

    Remember and keep this in the forefront of your thinking! *"We do not wrestle against flesh and blood but against the principalities, powers, against the rulers of darkness of this age and against spiritual hosts of wickedness in the heavenly places".* Ephesians 6:12 Also, remember, these spirits must have a physical body to operate in the earth realm. These demonic spirits requested that Jesus send them into the swine. I believe they wanted to remain in the region and continue to operate in this region. Jesus had to have a physical body to operate in the earth otherwise; He would not have been able to cast out these demonic spirits. Jesus gives the spirits permission (He is using His power legally) and the swine are destroyed in the body of water.

I cannot help but believe the anointing upon Jesus's life literally destroyed the yoke of bondage in this man's life. For Isaiah 10:27 says *it shall come to pass in that day this his burden will be taken away from your shoulder and his yoke from your neck; and the yoke will be destroyed because of the anointing oil. "* True and lasting deliverance will only take place when we use the correct spiritual warfare protocols.

Satan is a hard taskmaster and his burden will be destroyed when you are set free!

There will be times when we will be confronted with many spirits looking to oppress us, but we must learn to depend on the Holy Spirit to help us discern which spirit activity is present. I Corinthians chapter 12 lists the manifestations of the Holy Spirit, one of which is the *gift of discernment.* It is our responsibility as believers to learn to lean and depend on the Holy Spirit for help when we find ourselves helpless. John 14:26 says *"the Helper, the Holy*

Spirit whom the Father will send in my name, He will teach you all things and bring to your remembrance all things that I said to you". He is the great teacher, who knows all things, about everything.

Jude 1 states we should build ourselves up on our most holy faith by praying in the Holy Spirit. We are *Pretty Women,* who are powerful and who walk in the authority of Christ. You as a woman of God are valuable in the Kingdom. Look yourself in the mirror and tell yourself you are of great value; *you are God's Pretty Woman!* He has given you His weapons of warfare that are not carnal but mighty to pull down every stronghold, to be effective, to be whole, and to have healthy self-esteem.

I want to go back to discuss a segment of the movie *"Pretty Woman,"* which shows Vivian and Edward mutually being drawn together. The couple's togetherness is because they are similarly alike in moral character. Edward in part of his dialogue tells Vivian they are quite similar in that he seduces people to acquire their businesses. On the other hand, Vivian uses seduction to acquire their money for her services rendered.

We are talking about the spirit of harlotry, and one of the spirits that plague many women is the spirit of seduction. I want to lay a foundation that will allow you to see these actions and behaviors, and how God has a plan for our deliverance.

Seduction is a strong spirit that lures people into places they really thought they would never go. They become intoxicated with the thrill of the seduction so much so that they feel at home and comfortable in the place they have ventured. They become entangled much as a spider entangles his victim once they fall prey to the silky glistening web. When you fall into this web of entanglement, one becomes trapped and is unable to free his or herself.

The enemy uses such attraction to pervert the truth. It originates out of the soulish realm. All of this activity comes out of our soulish realm, which is our mind, will and emotions. Usually we find that lust and cravings will be the driving forces. I can remember a situation in my own life where I was being driven by a craving for some of my favorite candy. Now this might seem harmless and unrelated to what I am talking about, but believe me when I tell you that Satan tried to use this craving to destroy some relationships and my physical health.

One night I had to come to terms with my addiction. You see, I had been visiting a close friend and we were sitting around the kitchen table playing a game of spades with other friends in ministry. We were having a great time laughing and enjoying each other's company when a suggestion was made that we send someone to the store to purchase each of our favorite snacks. A list was made of everything that each of us requested. My friend decided that I did not need the candy I wanted and she proceeded to tell the person not to bring me any. I interrupted the conversation, said "no" in a rather stern voice, and proceeded to say that I did not need anyone speaking on my behalf. Since this conversation took place in jest, I assumed all was well and the person left for the store with the list in hand. There was caramel popcorn; vanilla ice cream; cookies; potato chips; soda and my favorite candy. We were playing cards, joking, and still having fun when our snacks arrived for our enjoyment.

Let me tell you I was really looking forward to eating my favorite snack. You see I had a special way that I enjoyed them. I would empty them all out and group them together by color. Each color represented a specific flavor; yellow was lemony; red was cherry; green was a lime flavor and then there was the berry flavors. Before I would eat them I would group them in special flavors so that I could get that burst of flavor in my mouth; I would pair the lemon with the cherry or the berry with the lime etc. always trying to achieve that unique burst of sweet and sour explosion flavor in my mouth. It was mouth-watering to say the least. This candy came in various flavors by packages and I loved them all. I loved this candy so much everyone who knew me would give me jars and tins of it as gifts because of my love for these little mouth pleasers.

Well, to make a long story short, when everyone was handed his or her snack, my snack was nowhere to be found. I questioned the individual as to why they chose to leave my snack in the store and the response was, because my friend told them not to get them. Now mind you, **everyone** had his or her favorite snack, including my friend! I did not! I was livid and upset! I immediately put away "my happy face and my mild mannered self" and stormed out of the house in search for my candy. I needed to have this candy and I wanted it at that moment! My mouth was watering for those Skittles. I was being driven and I had made such a scene. I was embarrassed but not embarrassed enough not to drive myself to the store to get those Skittles to satisfy my addiction. I was like an addict needing a fix! When I found the candy aisle, I was ready to put my hand on the bag when I heard the Lord in an audible voice say to me "Joanne you are being driven." "This has nothing to do with you wanting candy as much as it has to do with a spirit that is trying to destroy your physical health." I was scared at the sound of His voice, but I came to myself and understood the attack of

Satan who was trying to gain access through my health. The way I was eating this candy was frightening. I would always have a bag at work, in the car, and in my handbag. I did not want to be without them. I was instantly delivered and I am no longer a "candy" addict. Satan is cunning and he is subtle. My advice to you; is to keep the doors closed!

I want to go back to our two characters that I found rather alluring. Vivian is very beautiful, but hides her real beauty under the guise of a blond cheap wig and distasteful clothing. Edward is very handsome, and hides behind his power and influence on those who serve him and serve his money. What is interesting is that they are both driven and their drives are very destructive. However, at the very core of who they are, there is a moral goodness that has been covered up by disappointment in relationships and they have yielded to their perversion. She states when she does a "trick" she has become so numb to the process that it no longer bothers her, she is totally disengaged. He on the other hand confesses he is much like the same when he transacts his business acquisitions; he is detached from the process.

Vivian and Edward were detached because they were comfortable in their lifestyle position. In other words, they were both seduced by the spirit of seduction. They had become detached from their reality. Satan will use this strategy on us when we find ourselves empty and vulnerable. God asked me a question when thinking about Edward and Vivian. He asked; have we become numb to His presence? I ask you the same question. Have you become numb to the presence of God? Are you just going through the motions? Do you want more of God and all He has for you?

The Spirit of Divination

Acts 16:16-18, *Now it happened as we went prayer, that a certain slave girl possessed with a "spirit of divination," met us, who brought her masters much profit by fortune telling. This girl followed Paul and us and cried out saying, "These men are the servants of the Most High God, who proclaim to us the way of salvation." This religious spirit is the same spirit that had tormented and oppressed the man at Gadarenes in Mark 5. This she did for many days but Paul greatly annoyed turned and said to the spirit, (Paul separates the girl from the spirit, just like Jesus did when he commanded the demonic spirits of Legion to loose the man at Gadarenes) Paul commands the spirit to come out of her; "in the name of Jesus Christ come out of*

55

her!" And he came out that very hour. Paul is walking in the authority that Jesus had delegated to the believers.

God Jehovah Gibbor, the Mighty God of War, who teaches our hand to war and our fingers to fight says to us, *"be strong in the Lord (be strong in me) and in the power of His might, (my strength and ability) put on the my Armor that you may be able to stand against the wiles of the devil."* The word <u>wiles</u> means to be artful or beguiling. The behavior is deceptive. It also refers to a trick strategy meant to trap or entice, Vivian was engaged in rendering "tricks" to her clients and had become numb and detached from the process. She was oppressed by the spirit of seduction, and seduced as the young woman in Acts 16. Vivian was a slave in the market of prostitution. She thought she was in control of her own life and destiny but in actuality, she was in bondage to Satan. Satan was her Pimp. The spirit of witchcraft, which includes fortune-telling, horoscopes, palm and tealeaf readings; are all design by Satan to mimic the power of the Holy Spirit and the manifestation of the word of knowledge, word of wisdom and the gift of discernment. Satan has nothing of his own that is original. Satan will always pervert what is pure and Holy in your life if he finds an opening. We must learn how to operate effectively using prayer and our weaponry to wage war against Satan and his cohorts. By putting on our armor, we will be able to stand against the wiles of the devil and defeat him. We are all equipped to have victory over Satan if we use our weapons effectively. Let me remind you again, Luke 10:19 says ***God has given us power over all the power of our enemies.***

Paul was able to discern the spirit, identify the spirit, and cast the spirit out of the young woman and set the young woman free. We have the same power. Mark 16:17 tells us that these signs shall follow those who believe: In my name they will cast out demons and they will speak with new tongues. We must

> *God has given us power over all the power of our enemies*
> *Luke 10:19*

believe that we have the power and that demon spirits are subject to us through the name of Jesus. We have been commissioned to cast out devils and the Lord will work with us to confirm his word through accompanying signs

Pretty Woman

Chapter Three:

The Spirits of J. A. D.

Ecclesiastes chapter 4, verse: 12 *says;* though one may be overpowered by another, two can withstand him, and a threefold cord is not quickly or easily broken. This threefold cord represents God the Father, the Son, and the Holy Spirit. In the natural, a threefold cord cannot be severed very easily because it is intricately intertwined together for great strength. Likewise, in the spiritual application of this scripture, the threefold cord of the Godhead is intertwined for great might and great strength. It is impossible for Satan or demonic activity to overpower their strength.

Satan always finds ways to mimic God's kingdom and is the mastermind of his own threefold cord, **which I have dubbed** as the spirits of J.A.D. These spirits work together to try to entangle us, bind us to our past, and try to keep us from our future. They are the spirit of Jezebel, Athaliah, and Delilah. They create a powerful alliance to destroy God's people. They implement a spiritual force that blocks and aborts expansion, prevents breakthroughs and restricts our freedom. These are beautiful women, whose beauty is compared to that of Esther and Sarah. Though they had outward beauty and were hard to resist, they were wicked and devious in all of their dealings.

It is my hope as we identify spirit activities in the lives of selected Biblical characters, we will also identify these same spirits in our own behavior as well as others. God has given us great ability to master these spirits as we have seen in the study thus far. Remember, God the greatest, is on the inside of us and He is Jehovah Gibbor, the Mighty Man of War, who teaches our hands to war and our fingers to fight.

The Spirit of Jezebel

Jezebel is a heathen princess who came from a family of idol worshippers. I Kings 16: 30-31 states; *Now Ahab the son of Omri did evil in the sight of the Lord, more than all who were before him. And it came to pass, as though it had been a trivial thing for him to walk in the sins of Jeroboam the son of Nebat that he took as wife Jezebel the daughter of Ethbaal, king of the Sidonians; and he went and served Baal and worshiped him.* Ahab who was not only treacherous, and wicked than his predecessors, but his marriage to Jezebel positioned them to align their powers to rule more wickedly than all of their predecessors in each family's lineage. This powerful alliance formed through marriage is also the backdrop for the manifestation for many more treacherous deeds in their kingdom. History paints Ahab as a weak man in the natural, and he is easily influenced by his Queen. Jezebel usurps the authority and influence of her husband and becomes the ruling power of this union. Jezebel's behavior and her characteristics give permission for the spirits of seduction, manipulation, and control. The spirit of Jezebel is a seductive method that is used by prostitutes to entice their subjects into compromising in any area of their lives. The spirit of Jezebel operates in an illegitimate authority to seize our inheritance, as she did when she stole one man's vineyard; invited him to be an honored guest and then had him accused of blasphemy for which he was put to death by stoning. Her spirit inflicts poverty, spirits of infirmity; witchcraft activity and will manifest as a spirit of religion. Other offshoots of her activity would be confusion, disorientation, fear, manipulation, doubt, and double mindedness. The spirit of Jezebel always wants to create a stronghold in the lives of her victims. Jezebel manifests as a religious spirit, which operated in the young slave woman forced to work as a fortune-teller in Act 16. The spirit of religion looks like a relationship with the Father. It is easy to fall prey to a mindset of thinking that just because I fast and pray; lead the praise team; attend Bible study and participate in many good things in the church, that I have a relationship with the Lord based upon these outward works. *Matthew 15: 8 says these people draw near to me with their mouth and honor me with their lips but their heart is far from me.* We have seen this type of behavior in our churches. It appears as true worship, but the behavior on display denies the power of God to be demonstrated through pure worship, holy and righteous living.

Below are the following verses of scripture found in Revelation 2: 18-22, regarding the spiritual activity of Jezebel:

The Spirit of Jezebel is referenced in Revelation 2:18-23 And to the angel of the church in Thyatira write,

18 "These things says the Son of God, who has eyes like a flame of fire, and His feet like fine brass."

19 I know your works, love, service, faith, and your patience; and as for your works, the last are more than the first.

20 Nevertheless I have a few things against you, because you allow that woman Jezebel, who calls herself a prophetess, to teach and seduce My servants to commit sexual immorality and eat things sacrificed to idols.

21 And I gave her time to repent of her sexual immorality, and she did not repent.

22 Indeed I will cast her into a sickbed, and those who commit adultery with her into great tribulation, unless they repent of their deeds.

23 I will kill her children with death, and all the churches shall know that I am He who searches the minds and hearts. And I will give to each one of you according to your works.

The Church at Thyatira was found operating under the influence of Jezebel, the prophetess who teaches and seduces God's people to engage in sexual immorality and idol worship. This is a corrupt Church.

Queen Jezebel was guilty of introducing Baal worship to the children of Israel and still uses her influence today. She is passionate about her idol worship and has no fear of God or man. God, Jehovah Kanna, is a very jealous God and He commanded us not to bow down to any graven images or fashion gods to serve them. Jezebel's worship was toward Baal and she made that the religion of her kingdom. Her spirit is still very much alive. John the Baptist, the forerunner of Jesus had the ministry assignment of preparing the way for the "message of the kingdom." This message was (and continues to be) the gospel of Christ," to be preached and received. We can see how his message challenged the thinking of "religious leaders" among the Pharisees and Sadducees. John was met with great resistance, preaching his message and was ultimately put to death. This spirit was a religious spirit that looked like pious worship but was nothing more than works of flesh and doctrinal dogma. Because they were bound by the law, they did not want to exchange their traditions to embrace the truth. The spirit of religion is hypocritical and wrapped in legalism. The word is heard but the word is not applied to daily living. If we are not careful, we too will hold onto old beliefs, mindsets, and refuse, resist, reject and renounce truth to stay in bondage to doctrine and traditions and continue to worship buildings, personalities, and ministries. That is exactly one of the goals of the **spirit of Jezebel**. This spirit wants to create a stronghold of idolatry in us!

Queen Jezebel was a master of manipulation. Jezebel continues to use her influence by oppressing individuals with a controlling spirit and a spirit of intimidation. This usually is prevalent in relationships where there is low self-esteem and manifest as co-dependent behavior. These individuals are usually full of fear and are oblivious to their bondage and captivity. They are led to believe their relationship is based upon loyalty."

Queen Jezebel used manipulation and intimidation to remove Naboth from his inheritance, which was a vineyard. The Bible tells us that Ahab wanted his vineyard but Naboth would not sell it to him. Ahab told Queen Jezebel and Jezebel arranged for Naboth to be accused of blasphemy, which assured that he would be stoned to death. Her prowess was both devious and wicked. I Kings 21.

Queen Jezebel is a Murderer and releases the spirit of murder to influence her victims to operate from a place of violence and rage. Cain murdered Abel because of jealousy; Egypt's Pharaoh murdered all the Hebrews' male seed because they were multiplying and he was afraid the Egyptians would be overtaken. Moses in a fit of rage murdered an Egyptian slave trying to resolve a dispute. In I Kings 18:3 we read that Jezebel was responsible for killing God's prophets in retaliation to Elijah having slaughtered her 450 Prophets of Baal that served in her court and at her pleasure. She instilled fear in Elijah when Ahab told Jezebel everything Elijah had done and how he had executed all the prophets with the sword. Jezebel sent a messenger to Elijah to say, "May the gods deal with me, be it ever so severely, if by this time tomorrow I do not make your life like that of one of them." Elijah was afraid and ran for his life. The spirit of Jezebel will boldly confront us and we must not succumb to the taunting and harassments. It is interesting to me that the Lord allows us to see the vulnerability of His servants. That should be a comfort to us that there will be times in our lives when we will find ourselves running away from situations that confront us and we will cry out to the Father for His protection!

David said *"deliver me O Lord from evil men; preserve me from the violent men who plan evil things in their hearts,"* Psalm 140:1-2. This certainly can be our prayer when we find ourselves afraid!

Fear will release the presence of Satan, the kingdom of darkness. Faith releases the presence of God, the kingdom of light. When we embrace fear, faith will not operate. Satan and his demon hosts will have legal right to steal, kill, and destroy. Remember, fear is an intimidating spirit that tries to open a door of access that will allow spirits to operate within us. Faith should be our first reaction when we are faced with difficult situations or tragic news.

The Spirit of Athaliah

The histories of these spirits are very important, because in order for us to rid ourselves as well as others from their activity, we must be able to uproot them going back to the third and fourth generation. As we delve into the origin of the spirit of Athaliah, we will see how this spirit is power hungry and wants to rule at all cost by destroying generations of families or generations of dynasties. Athaliah can and will utilize the spirit of witchcraft to help accomplish her goal. My goal in this chapter is to help you identify this type of activity in your family and in other relationships.

Second Kings 8:16-26, tells us that Jehoram was the firstborn son of Jehoshaphat. Jehoram began his reign as king of Judah while still in his father's household. Jehoshaphat was a good king who sought and obeyed God. His relationship with God was founded upon trust and obedience. He relied on God to deliver him from the hands of his enemies. Jehoram was a witness of the victories they enjoyed while reining alongside his father.

At the age of thirty-two years old during his eighth year of reign, the scripture tells us that Jehoram began to walk in the ways of the kings of Israel, as the house of Ahab had done for he married a daughter of Ahab. Let me say again;

He was the "seed" of a righteous King but because he yielded to the spirit of seduction that operated in Athaliah, the daughter of Ahab and Jezebel, the granddaughter of Omri, he then became as evil as his predecessors did.

We have the responsibility to train our children in the way they should go. Training a child Biblically does not mean our children will not go astray or make detrimental decisions which may ultimately destroy God's plans for their lives. Adam and Eve made a disastrous decision that affected all of mankind. However, thanks be to God, for redemption and reconciliation. With our children, keep praying, keep speaking the word over your children, and cover your children with the blood of Jesus. God, our Father is a covenant keeping God, keeping covenant to His children from generation to generation

Now as was the case with Jezebel and Ahab, the marriage of Jehoram and Athaliah also formed a powerful alliance and would ultimately have a foothold to operate and influence Jehoshaphat's decisions to seek the help of Ahab and Ahaziah in the future. Nevertheless, for the sake of His servant David, the LORD was not willing to destroy Judah. He had promised to maintain a lamp for David and his descendants forever. The Lord had a covenant with David. His seed shall endure forever and his throne as the sun.

We too can take comfort in knowing these words of our Father God that His loving-kindness *He will not utterly take from us; nor allow His faithfulness to fail. He will not break His covenant with you and me. Nor will He alter His word to us once He has spoken. His word to us shall be established forever like the moon, even like the faithful witness in the sky. "Selah."* (Pause and meditate on this for a minute) **Psalms 89:34-38.**

We can be assured that if our children go astray, like God's children; Adam and Eve faltered, the promises that He has made to us regarding our seed will hold true. Do not give up on your children. Let me reiterate, do not stop praying for your children when they have gone astray and living contrary to their upbringing. If you are not praying for your children begin to pray over them now. It does not matter how old your children are! Pray that they will be taught of the Lord, and they are learning to listen for the voice of God like Samuel who was taught to distinguish the voice of God above the voice of man. Pray that the eyes of their understanding are being opened. Come against the spirit of rebellion and hedge them in like Hosea hedged-in Gomer to prevent her from seeking and finding those spirits that had her affection.

Athaliah was no doubt attracted to Jehoram because of his weakness, much like her father Ahab. Once married, Athaliah's seductive influences manipulated Jehoram into introducing Baal worship in Judah. This introduction to Baal set in motion the spirit of murder to be unleashed in their family. When Jehoram is given full reign of the kingdom from his father King Jehoshaphat, the scripture states *"he strengthened himself and slew all of his six brothers for their inheritance which was silver and gold and fenced in cities of Judah."* *2 Chronicles 21:1-7.*

Jehoram and Athaliah continued the dynasty of wickedness by producing a son named Ahaziah who at age twenty-two years became king for one year. He walked in the ways of his parents and wicked grandfather Ahab and continued doing evil in the eyes of the LORD. These generations became more and more evil from one generation to the next displaying more and more wicked behavior.

I hope you are beginning to see how the seed of this family has a genetic coding of wickedness and evil, which was passed from one generation to another. Jezebel is the daughter of Ethbaal, an idol worshipper, Ahab is the son of Omri, an idol worshipper, and they begat Athaliah, an idol worshipper. Athaliah was married to Jehoram and was the granddaughter of Omri. Their union produces an heir named

Ahaziah, an idol worshipper. The influence in Ahaziah is so strong by his mother Athaliah, the cycle of wickedness and idolatry is perpetuated. However, it is clear that the ruling spirits and principality had become a stronghold in her bloodline, lineage, and each successive generation from these unions.

A seed will always reproduce after its own kind. This is a spiritual law whether applied to the natural realm or applied to the spiritual realm

Athaliah, the seed of Jezebel becomes more wicked and devious than her mother does.

The spirit of Athaliah is destined to destroy generations and generational blessings. The demonic force of Athaliah releases a more intense attack of false prophecy, witchcraft, and divination. She blocks your breakthroughs with her evil seductive words causing doubt regarding God's promise of destiny, as that spirit did in the Garden of Eden with Adam and Eve.

In the book of Genesis, we note that it was God's intent to restore the relationship between Himself and His creation as well as the relationship between Adam and Eve. Remember Adam blamed the woman for the influence she had over him and his decision to disobey God. What we should understand about the "temptation" was that it was Satan who **manifested** as **the spirit of seduction** in the Garden of Eden whose attempt was to have a relationship with mankind, equal to this relationship that God had with His creation. The only way for this to happen was for Satan to legally find an open door to man. Satan was a "fallen angel" who was separated from God because of his lust for power. He was prideful and hungry for the kingdom of God. Isaiah 14:2 says, *"How you are fallen from heaven, O Lucifer, son of the morning! How you are cut down to the ground, you who weakened the nations!"*

13 For you have said in your heart: 'I will ascend into heaven, I will exalt my throne above the stars of God; I will also sit on the mount of the congregation on the farthest sides of the north;

14 I will ascend above the heights of the clouds; I will be like the Most High.'

15 Yet you shall be brought down to Sheol, to the lowest depths of the Pit.

His domain was the second heaven, which was the earth before God created the Garden of Eden for His creation called humanity, which would evolve, from Adam and Eve.

God declares to us after the "fall of mankind," how He would bring about restoration and how He would reconcile and redeem His creation. Just as God loved Adam and Eve, God loves us. The Bible says that while we are yet in our sin or fallen state Christ would die for us. What a picture of His unconditional love for you and me. Why wouldn't we make him the "object of our affection?" God, Jehovah Kanna, our Lover, my Lover always has a plan of restoration and redemption after our fall. He said, "I will put animosity between you and the woman, and between your descendant and her descendant; (or between the seed of God and the seed of Satan); he will bruise your head, and you will bruise his heel." The heel represents "our walk" or "our lifestyle" based upon choices we make according to the knowledge or truth, facts that we embrace. Satan would be allowed to cause man to stumble.

God intended for the woman to be redeemed and exalted. Now let me be clear and say that a woman was never going to be exalted to rule over a man but her position was going to be restored to being a co-heir of the earth realm. Her power to rule and reign in the earth and have dominion was going to be given back to her. God's seed would bruise the "head." Let's think about what the "head" represents. The head represents the center of thinking as well as power and authority. Deuteronomy 28:13 says *the Lord will make you the head and not the tail; you shall be above only, and not be beneath, if you heed the commandments of the Lord your God.* The head contains the brain, eyes, ears, nose, and mouth. This is the control center for intellect, thoughts, memory, mind, understanding, and emotions. Our five senses are controlled by the head. In other words, God's plan was to restore dominion or to give the power to govern back to His children. God used the casing of flesh for His seed to be birthed in the earth realm, because he had to have the body of a woman to accomplish that goal legally.

Second Chronicles 22:1-12 and 2 Kings 11: 1-3 tells us that Athaliah was so power hungry and driven by her quest to sit on the throne and rule Judah that after she hears about her son's Ahaziah's death, she rises to power and murders her own grandsons; the royal heirs to her son's throne. She destroys her seed and lineage, with the exception of one named Joash who was hidden by his nanny. Joash took his rightful place on the throne of David to rule Judah. This was God's covenant promise to David being fulfilled.

Because of the covenant God had with David, he would not pass judgment against Ahaziah. When Ahaziah visits with his sick cousin then God chooses to use this occasion to deal with his wickedness and sin. All of the seed of Ahab was destroyed to pass judgment against the missteps of Jehoshaphat's alliance with Ahab. Remember earlier in our reading, (II Kings 8: 19), God's hand was stayed upon the house of Jehoshaphat while he was alive. After his death God's judgment is released. We can be sure that the wages of sin is always death. Whether in the physical sense or whether in the spiritual sense; to sin is to die.

This was the third time that the spirit of Athaliah tried to destroy the seed of David. But, God intervenes by elevating "the woman" to preserve the seed and lineage of Jesus. He uses Moses' mother in her wisdom to hide Moses from being destroy. He uses Rahab, a prostitute to save her household and to become a part of the bloodline and lineage of Jesus. Just as Athaliah's spirit was active in biblical days, this spirit is still wielding influence in the earth today. Her spirit will always try to manifest to usurp authority, rise to power and destroy generations. In some families, you will see a history of a sickness or disease that is prevalent from one generation to the next. Often, the death rate within a family is high from one generation to the next. This activity can be influenced by the spirit of Athaliah.

Let's look at how this spirit destroyed other generations. The **spirit of Athaliah** was prevalent in the following events:

- Pharaoh decreed all the Hebrew males to be destroyed; but Moses was kept alive by his mother. Pharaoh's daughter raised him as her son. Acts 7:17-22.

- King Herod operated under the influence of the spirit of Athaliah. He ordered all male children under the age of two to be killed, hoping to destroy the seed of Jesus. The spirit of Athaliah came through a door of jealousy according to Matthew 2:16.

- Hitler during the holocaust of the Jewish people promoted genocide. Families were destroyed, and the door of hatred opened. Hitler had a lust for power, he wanted to rule the whole world.

- Rwandan genocide; the spirit of Athaliah opened the door of witchcraft and the occult. The Hutu's had a lust for power, one-hundred days of killing and eradicating of families.

- The Kennedy brothers, Joseph Jr., John, Robert, John Jr. all met with untimely deaths, the Spirit of Athaliah, door of pride; idolatry; infidelity.

We must not be ignorant about identifying this kind of activity in our lives, the lives of others, or our families. We must use our authority over the spirit of Athaliah when we see it trying to manifest. God has given us power over all the power of Satan (Luke 10:19, Mark 16). God will co-labor with us to see a manifestation of His power and deliverance. Praise God!

The Spirit of Delilah

Delilah is the third spirit that makes up the three-fold cord of Satan's powerful alliance. Delilah was an evil seducer more so than Jezebel and Athaliah. She lived close to the area where Jezebel was born and was probably influenced by the same spirit and seductive tendencies. She was beautiful and irresistible, and was an idol worshiper as well.

Delilah's name means languish, and her character reflected her weakness. She was a weak woman, who took money from the lords of the Philistines to gain information from Samson regarding his strength, in order to diminish Samson's power. The spirit of Delilah is also seductive, but this spirit takes it time, coming to you little by little in order to rob you of your spiritual strength.

Delilah's name is translated as delicate. The root meaning of the name is "to be brought low, to hang down and to be languid." Languid means slow, lifeless, weak, lacking in spirit or interest. Our word languish comes from this root word. Thus, her name indicates Delilah would weaken and bring down Samson. Their story is found in Judges 16:1-31.

Samson opened the door to be seduced by the spirits of seduction and spirit of harlotry by engaging in fornication in chapter fifteen. Verse 1 states; he went to Gaza (Hebrew word for Gaza means fortified and strong) and saw a harlot there and went in to her. Samson and the city of Gaza had great strength and fortitude. There was a natural attraction. In other words, he joins himself and he becomes a part of the spirit of harlotry. He gives permission for the spirit to operate in his life, and he is literally forming a soul tie with this spirit, which will ultimately destroy him. Satan seeks opportunities to establish a well-fortified place in our weaknesses or places of vulnerability to build and establish a stronghold. Spirits always seek to inhabit a body to operate. These spirits must have a legitimate place of residence in order to operate while in the earth or atmosphere.

After Samson's encounter with the harlot, he travels to the <u>Valley of Sorek</u> where Delilah lives and we are told he is taken by her beauty and falls in love with her.

When we speak of the Valley of Sorek; the Hebrew word is "Ge" which means "a bursting" and "a flowing together," a narrow glen or ravine. This valley was very fertile. In other words, Delilah's low self-esteem has her living from a "low place." This is fertile ground for spirits looking for a place to take up residence. Whenever Satan sees his fruits, his tendencies, his behaviors he will come right in and begin to rule and reign. In this case, Delilah has given place to the spirit of Jezebel as they flow together. A powerful alliance is formed for Satan's strategy to work and overtake his prey.

Delilah is not a murderer like Jezebel and Athaliah, but she is motivated by the love of money, which invites the spirit of mammon to manifest and operate.

The Philistines were looking for an occasion to inflict revenge on Samson for slaughtering one thousand of their own men. Delilah is the pawn to accomplish this goal as we read the story. The Philistine lords approach Delilah and say "Entice Samson and find out where his great strength lies and by what means we may overpower him, that we may <u>BIND him to AFFLICT him</u> and each of us will give you eleven hundred pieces of silver." The word "entice" used in this context means to allure, deceive, or persuade in a sinister way. In other words, the Philistine lords wanted her to use the power of seduction to bring him down and make him weak. The Philistines hated Samson's strength and wanted to bind Samson much like the strongman of the Gadarenes found in Mark 5 who had many demons operating within him. The many demons referred as Legion, bound and afflicted. Satan too, wants to use many spirits to promote his activity to bind, imprison, afflict, oppress, or humble us. He then will have legal right to steal, kill, and destroy in our lives and our circumstances. Satan's job description will never change, he is in the earth to steal, kill, and destroy wherever and whenever he can dominate.

Satan uses Delilah to steal Samson's strength and to redirect his passion for God. Her beauty and delicate nature made her seduction irresistible. However, the true reality is that she is a seductress who wanted to destroy Samson's destiny. The spirit of Athaliah is her true nature.

Delilah begins pestering him daily with her words and presses him so that his soul was vexed to death. The spirit of seduction though subtle becomes aggressive and confrontational. Samson finally yields and reveals all that is in his heart; he shares the secret to his strength. He says, "No razor has ever come upon my head for I have been a Nazirite to God from my mother's womb. If I am shaven, then my strength will leave me and <u>I shall become weak</u> and be like any other man." The spirit of seduction has overpowered him and reduced Samson, a man of great strength to mere putty in its clutches. Persistence has a way of penetrating the soul of the heart, and will cause one to yield to the spirit of seduction.

Samson was considered a spiritual Hercules, who was courageous and used by God against the enemies of God. Yet Delilah, controlled by the powerful spirit alliances of Athaliah and Jezebel, with the outward manifestation of the spirit of seduction, successfully reduces Samson to weakness. Delilah accomplished this by lulling Samson to a deep sleep while his head was in her lap. By putting his head in the enemies lap, Samson gave his enemy the power to influence his thoughts and the way he would think. He is no longer in control of how he thinks because he has been beguiled by the seductress Delilah. Once in captivity he was put to shame and humiliation and brought low in the sight of all who observed his decline. She accomplished the goal of the Philistines in making him weak, thereby taking his strength, and draining the life out of Samson. At times Satan will be strategic in targeting God's strongest warriors much in the same way to use this tactic and unleashing his seducing spirits **to strip** them of their power and strength. I say to all of my sisters, "be strong in the Lord, and put on the whole armor of God to stand against all the wiles of the devil, your adversary." Stand against Satan with the power and might of God to pull down all of the strongholds in your life. Remember the weapons of your warfare are not carnal; they are not weak but mighty. You can do it! I was reminded in Genesis 39: 1-23, that the spirits of Delilah and Athaliah tried to work together to seize Joseph's destiny. They would manifest themselves whenever Joseph was in Potiphar's house tending to his daily tasks. Potiphar's wife lusted after Joseph day after day and would repeatedly make advances toward Joseph. Her advancements toward Joseph were purely sexual in nature. Joseph who had respect for himself and God resisted the temptation to fulfill her lust. His reply is amazing for a young man; with strong convictions and moral standing Joseph refuses to sin against God. I surmise that maybe 1 Thessalonians 4:3-5 came to mind. *"For this is the will of God your sanctification that you should abstain from sexual immorality, that each of you should know how to possess his own vessel in sanctification and honor not in passion of lust, like the heathen who do not know God."*

These spirits were unsuccessful because Joseph was grounded and rooted in his relationship with the Lord. He had respect for himself and God and was able to resist the temptation to fulfill her lust. He was strong in the Lord and in the power of His might. He had his armor on.

My Personal Testimony

I want to share a personal testimony with you. My testimony is to allow you to see just how a powerful alliance of spirits can influence decisions that are made in one's life unknowingly. It is crucial that we learn to identify spirit activity because when they identify a weakness, and find an open portal, they will devise an attack. In terms of the three-fold cord of Satan, these spirits are gender neutral, and they are formed to wage warfare against all and any who will give them permission, whether knowingly or unknowingly. Yes, that is exactly right; we can be blind to behavior within ourselves that invite them in our lives to influence our decisions. These spirits intend to build a stronghold permanently in your life. It is possible for them to overpower the strong or the weak.

In 1978, I was truly excited that I was going to have another child. I had a good pregnancy and even convinced myself I was going to have another daughter, a baby girl. My thoughts were always on how she would look and how I had planned to dress her. At that time, the sonograms were not as they are today, where the gender of your baby could be revealed. The results of the sonogram did not support what I had conjured up in my mind about this pregnancy. When I gave birth, I was very upset and despondent when they told me I had a little boy. I did not know what I was going to do with this child. Still in disbelief, and sometimes delusional, I kept telling myself I am not a "boy mommy." I did not know what to do with little boys. I could not even relate to boys as I could to little girls. My husband on the other hand was ecstatic and elated. He was already planning a great future for his son that included fishing trips and "sons and dads stuff." When he came to visit, he would peep his head in the door to my room, which was not a warm and cozy atmosphere, as one would expect for a maternity wing. The hospital room was sterile and cold with space for two beds. I did not have a roommate so I was alone.

When visiting, my husband would say hello and ask how I was doing, but he would tell me he was on his lunch break and (only thirty minutes most days) he was going to visit the baby! He did not come to see me; he came to see the baby! Years ago when babies were born, they were kept in a separate area, and not allowed in your room. The only exception was if you were a breast-feeding mother. Every time he came to the hospital, he would say and do the same thing. To add injury to insult, the new mothers in my area wing had received these great big bouquets of flowers and balloons that said "Congratulations" on your baby girl or baby boy. I could not escape the jubilation, excitement, and visitations all around me as well as other husbands displaying such love, affection, and concern for their wives. This really bothered me because there was no outward display of love or concern for me. At that time, a normal pregnancy hospital admission would be three to four days, so needless to say, during my stay at the hospital I was feeling really unloved. As an afterthought, on the day of my discharge I received a single vase with one rose. I was not a happy camper and I am sure my face communicated my disappointment. My delivery was traumatic and complicated and all I get is a single rose! I grinned and smiled but I was thinking how insensitive. I am sure he had no clue!

My mind took me back to the delivery day; I could not help but remember how the epidural I was given did not take effect while I was in labor. I experienced so much pain, that it made it impossible for me to push this eight and one-half pound baby out, so the doctor had to use forceps to bring him out. I was so traumatized, every time they said "Mrs. Green," we need you to push, I looked at them and said this is so easy, you push! The delivery table I was on was cold and made of metal. There were no sheets to give me a sense of privacy for my private parts; I was naked for all the world to see and they are asking me to push! Between my son's head being big, and using forceps to get him out, I had a very large tear that needed thirteen stitches. I was not given any anesthesia or anything to numb the area while they sewed me up after removing the afterbirth. I was so glad to be going home at this point I just took that vase with the single rose and home I went but not without a plan.

This traumatic experience made me more determined not to have any more children. I was done. I was not going to go through that humiliation ever again in this lifetime. The shop was closed; nailed shut and I just kept taking my birth control pills. When asked why I could not get pregnant again, I just had no response; after all, it took me three years after our marriage to get pregnant with my son. I was sure my husband having come from a family of fourteen, wanted more children, but I had "closed the shop." In fact, three years later, unbeknownst to me, I opened the door for the "spirit of Delilah" to operate her influence of seduction. I pestered my husband, about getting a vasectomy, telling him that we should get this done while he was still in the military and while we had the medical benefits. When I saw that this tactic wasn't working I then began begging him to let me have my tubes tied, this went on for over a year and finally he gave in to my "pestering" and I had surgery to have my tubes tied. Finally, I could close this chapter of my life; after all, we had a girl and a boy. We should have been the perfect and happy little family of four!

Fast forward eleven years later, the fruit of the seed I planted manifested because of the wound I had received from lack of attention and love. My selfish attitude and vengeful spirit, allowed the door to be wide open for the spirit activity of this threefold cord of Jezebel, Athaliah and Delilah to manifest and operate. This powerful alliance waged warfare against us and loosed a spirit of division that had begun to operate in our home and what ensued was an environment of hostility and anger between us. I was never physically abused but felt mentally and emotionally abused with the words that were being hurled at me. My husband finally asked for a divorce and I believe that one reason I was being divorced was my decision not to have any more of "his" children. When we married, my daughter was four-years old and he adopted her, giving her his name, and by all accounts, he was a very good and loving Dad to her.

Before our son was born, my daughter was raised just like an only child, he spoiled her, and the bond between them was unbreakable. Now, not only was he going to divorce me but also he was going to file for custody of my son who at the time was only eight and a half years-old. My daughter, who was eighteen years old had a rebellious and troublesome teenage era and had a child out of wedlock, during this turbulent time. Under the influence by those around her, my daughter decided to take her child away from me and move to another state. Her hatred for me was being fueled and fed by these oppressive spirits. My family, my son, my daughter and husband had formed their own threefold cord, an alliance of their own to make me feel the sting of alienation in my own home. There was absolutely no communication in my house and it was just pure hell.

Sadly, not long after this tumultuous and turbulent time that ended in divorce, my daughter committed suicide. Again, let me say that we do not wrestle with flesh and blood but against principalities, against powers, against the rulers of darkness and against spiritual hosts of wickedness. Satan must have a legal right to steal, kill, and destroy.

I say all of this because, years later God showed me how I opened the door, how I gave permission for the cord of Satan, to operate as the spirits of Jezebel, Athaliah, and Delilah. These powerful alliances came to seduce; steal my family's inheritance and rob me of my relationship with my daughter by having her take her own life at the age of twenty-three years old. Remember, Jezebel used manipulation; I used manipulation in my relationship, Delilah used seduction by wearing Samson down with her words and with her seduction. I used seduction by wearing my husband down to allow me to have my tubes tied. Athaliah murdered her grandson's to wipe out her seed and therefore destroy her generations. The door was opened for that spirit to oppress my daughter, to move upon her to take her own life. It is so important to identify behavioral patterns in our own lives, the lives of our family members and those that we have relationship with to close those doors to these powerful alliances of the threefold cord of Satan. I want you to see in your own lives and personal events where doors might be open. It is my prayer, having shared this testimony; you are equipped and armed to take back any territory lost.

As Pretty Women, we must not allow anything in our past or present to lie dormant, to grow, and manifest giving way for these spirits to remain active or to become activated. We should not be brought under any condemnation from Satan, regarding choices we made today or in our past. I believe that the Father, Jehovah Kanna, our loving, and forgiving God wants to bring healing to those places He identifies as wounds, bruises or trauma. If we do not deal with these issues and trauma in our lives, as God reveals them to us, they become a stronghold, then the activity becomes intense, and that activity intensifies until it ends up destroying us. We will then continue to make bad and unwise decisions that are contrary to the destiny that God has for our lives and for the healing He wants to release to us.

I also want to say, if there are any of you who have had an abortion or abortions, you too can be free from condemnation and the tormenting spirits that have been harassing you. I sense that some of these abortions were driven in part by the spirit of Athaliah, and you were under great pressure to abort. I say to you today, our loving Father will blot out your transgression like a thick cloud, and separate you from the sin of murder and see you as his redeemed daughter, having gladly given Himself for you. God will not hold you in your past He wants to release you to a glorious, guilt free future!

Prayer:

Heavenly Father, it is my prayer today, that you lovingly and tenderly reveal to your women; who may be in the role of a daughter, a mother, a sister or wife who have been compelled to read this book, and by reading this book have come face to face with areas in their lives that have been laced with destructive patterns, and destructive cycles of behavior, that have kept them from loving themselves and from loving you. Create in them a deep hunger and thirst, that causes them to pant only after you. Fill to the full every empty place in their lives with your Awesome Presence.

I pray that the anointing released to them today, breaks and destroys all yokes of bondages that have manifested through manipulation and control, seduction and intimidation, murder or lust. Let them receive your power of forgiveness for themselves and embrace your grace to walk in that forgiveness. Let the power of your might strengthen them to be "pretty women" as they draw closer to you than they have ever been or they

could have ever imagined. In the mighty, powerful,
name of Jesus, the Christ, the Anointed One. Amen

Back to the movie, Vivian and Edward are being drawn to a place of comfort as they continue to engage with one another seductively and playfully. While having a serious discussion, Edward looks deeply into Vivian's soul and makes this assessment. He explains how much alike they really are by stating he seduces people for their businesses and she seduces people in exchange for their money. Seduction is a strong spirit that lures people into places they really thought they would never go. They become intoxicated with the thrill of the seduction so much so that they feel at home and comfortable at where they have ventured. They then become entangled much as a spider lures and entangles his victim once they fall prey to the cunningly crafted silky glistening web. They are trapped, unable to free themselves.

Any spirit will use certain attractions the enemy uses to pervert truth. It originates out of the soulish realm. Lust and cravings are the driving forces. I think that it is important to reiterate again that even though Edward had good looks, money, power, and influence and Vivian was beautiful, they were both hiding. She was hiding behind a cheap, blonde wig and he was hiding behind his wealth, power and influence which were things that are superficial in nature. Initially, for me, as I watched the movie, I could not detect their moral goodness because of their flagrant behavior. Edward and Vivian did not want to reveal their authentic selves. Because of failed relationships and disappointments they not only yielded to their perversion but were headed on a path of destruction. They both had become numb to the processes of doing "their" business. This assessment should force us to honestly address the question again; of whether or not, we too have become disengaged and numb in our relationship with God.

Have we become numb to the presence of a God who loves us so much that He gave Himself sacrificially for all of Eternity? Who loves us perfectly? Are we no longer emotionally moved to a place where we desperately want more of Him and all He has for us. Are we just going through the religious motions?

In my study of the Old Testament, I found that God likens His children (the children of Israel) to a harlot/prostitute. Out of sixty-six books of the Bible, God mentions harlots or harlotry in twenty-three books. It is clear then, that one third of the Bible's discussion is related to the spirit of harlotry.

Judges 2:17 says; *Yet they would not listen to their judges, but they played the harlot with other gods and bowed down to them. They turned quickly from the way in which their fathers walked, in obeying my commandments.*

Judges 8:33-35 says, *So it was, as soon as Gideon was dead, that the children of Israel again played the harlot with the Baals and made Baal-Berith their god.* Baal-Berth means a covenant lord. He was a god they worshipped in Shechem after the death of Gideon contrary to Jehovah Kanna's command. Jehovah Kanna means The Lord is Jealous.

Please, do not misunderstand me, I want us to keep our focus on the spirit of the harlotry, which is often depicted as an outcast from society but engaged in when there is an insatiable lust for fleshly enjoyment or when the flesh or carnal appetites must be fulfilled at any cost. In other words, the devil will shame and label you, but will use you when he has a need for you.

Only God can detect the real desires, hopes, or dreams of an outcast. Such was the case regarding two women; one found in the Old Testament and one in the New Testament. Their stories are written to remind us of God's covenant love toward His people. These women remind us that they were interwoven into God's sovereign plan of redemption to deliver mankind from deep rooted perverted sin.

Chapter Four:

The Harlot of Nain

There is a harlot, a prostitute in the City of Nain. the Pharisee's called her a sinner, (a woman labeled, no name but labeled with un-pleasantries), not addressed by a proper name only by a label, which Jesus should not allow any contact not to mention not even a touch. Why? The woman had a spirit of harlotry dictating her lifestyle. She who washed His feet with her tears, dried His feet with her hair, and anointed them with very expensive fragrant oils from her alabaster box. Jesus was her Savior. Luke 7:36-50

The backdrop for this story begins in Luke 7:11-17. The observations revealed through these scriptures tell us:

- Jesus was an invited guest,
- the Harlot of Nain was an intruder and an unwanted presence,
- a boy raised from the dead,
- great excitement in the City,
- a treasure within the Alabaster Box,
- a religious spirit manifest.

The miracle mentioned in Luke 7:11-17 is where our attention should focus:

11 Soon afterward, Jesus went to a town called Nain, and his disciples and a large crowd went along with him.

12 As he approached the town gate, a dead person was being carried out--the only son of his mother, and she was a widow. And a large crowd from the town was with her.

13 When the Lord saw her, his heart went out to her and he said, "Don't cry."

14 Then he went up and touched the coffin, and those carrying it stood still. He said, "Young man, I say to you, get up!"

15 The dead man sat up and began to talk, and Jesus gave him back to his mother.

16 They were all filled with fear and praised God. "A great prophet has appeared among us," they said. "God has come to help his people."

17 This news about Jesus spread throughout Judea and the surrounding country.

No doubt this harlot of Nain heard about this wonderful miracle. The Bible says fear had come upon all and they glorified God and said a great prophet had risen up among them. I believe that she knew in her heart that she wanted to meet this great man. I believe that she knew she "held a great treasure that would gain her entrance into his presence." Her expensive "oil" in an alabaster box that would be the envy of all who were already at the elaborate private feast, including any other prominent guest.

Matthew 26: 6-13

6 And when Jesus was in Bethany at the house of Simon the leper,

7 A woman came to Him having an alabaster flask of very costly fragrant oil, and she poured it on His head as He sat at the table.

8 But when His disciples saw it, they were indignant, saying, "Why this waste?"

9 For this fragrant oil might have been sold for much and given to the poor."

10 But when Jesus was aware of it, He said to them, "Why do you trouble the woman? For she has done a good work for me.

11 For you have the poor with you always, but me you do not have always.

12 For in pouring this fragrant oil on My body, she did it for My burial.

13 Assuredly, I say to you, wherever this gospel is preached in the whole world, what this woman has done will also be told as a memorial to her."

In Matthew 26:6-13 and Mark 14:3-9 the disciples' attend a dinner at Simon the leper's house. We have a Pharisee, the disciples, Jesus and the harlot, an intruder, and uninvited guest at the private dinner party.

Both accounts of what happened here focused on this woman's negligence of "wasting her expensive oil "on Jesus, the honored guest. Both accounts state, "they were indignant." In other words their feelings or their behavior was characterized by expressing strong displeasure, they were offended. Mark's account criticizes the woman sharply. Their offense is an open door for demonic activity to manifest. Jesus rebukes them and points out that her outward demonstration of anointing his head and the washing of His feet was to prepare His body for death. She was the "poor" and represented all who are poor in spirit. Isaiah 10:27 says: It shall come to pass in that day, that his burden will be taken away from your shoulder and his yoke from your neck, and the yoke will be destroyed because of the "anointing oil."

Using her oil symbolized the anointing of the Holy Spirit to break and destroy the yoke of death over the lives of all the Gentiles and sinners, those He came to save and deliver. Jesus came that he might destroy the works of Satan. She then becomes a benefactor of His forgiveness for her sins and His eternal salvation and she was freed from the yoke of bondage of her past sins and would have a bright new future.

Jesus says; and both accounts are written in red, "Assuredly, I say to you, wherever this gospel is preached in the whole world, what this woman has done will also be told as a memorial to her." Here is a harlot who now has been elevated to a place of prominence for the entire world to take note. This woman without significance now becomes significant. This woman would be forever remembered for her kind act of service.

Both accounts show us how easy it is for us, as believers to operate in a "religious spirit," having the form of godliness but denying its power (2 Timothy 3:5) The disciples and Simon focused on the external/natural display of the harlots work rather than the internal spiritual work that she was in desperate need of. Jesus, His focus was on his mandate, His mission to bring salvation to all who were lost regardless of their past lives or background.

Jesus extends an invitation to her. He makes her welcomed and acceptable in everyone's sight. She goes from a harlot, cloaked with the spirit of harlotry, living a sinful lifestyle to a redeemed woman, predestined to be in right standing with God. She was instantly made righteous. Her status changed from a woman whom those around her labeled a harlot, a sinner, a nobody to somebody that the whole world would come to know and recognize.

There will be times in our lives where the spirit within will draw us to a place where we are an uninvited guest. The Lord's anointing upon us will manifest to destroy the works of darkness, yokes will be destroyed, and the captives will be set free. My past might, and your past may label us as a harlot or a Pharisee. We might have judged others and walked in a religious spirit but despite our past, the Lord will extend His invitation to elevate us. Once elevated we will be recognized and known as a threat among the demons of Satan's kingdom. This scripture reinforces in my mind that the tangible anointing on our lives is valid. This anointing is used to set the captives free, destroy the works of darkness, and allow the Holy Spirit to uncover those things in our lives that may hinder our walk and limit the effectiveness of that anointing.

Her story is recorded in the three gospels, Matthew, Mark, and Luke. Luke, the physician gives us an account of her story from his medical point of view and his observation reminds us, that all who are sick are in need of the Great Physician. All who are facing eternal death can have eternal life if we accept Jesus's invitation. The harlot bowed at the feet of Jesus to worship and brought Him her best gift. Her gift to Him was her broken, unfulfilled, sinful life, what an exchange! A Pretty Women, redeemed by promise predestined for purpose!

Chapter Five:

Rahab's Story

Rahab, a Type of the Gentile Church

Rahab's story is found in Joshua 6:17-25. She hid the messengers whom Joshua sent to spy out Jericho, before they overtook the city to destroy it. Rahab and her household were spared from destruction by the command of Joshua (Jehovah the Savior).

Her story begins in chapter two of Joshua. What we know about Rahab is that she was a prostitute/harlot who was a Gentile in the Canaanite city of Jericho. Jericho was one of the principal places of idol worship. Ashtoreth was the Goddess of the Moon and all that was vile and degrading was very evident and prevalent. It would be safe to say, that the spirit of Jezebel and Delilah was very active. Rahab's name means "the proud one," so she was not only known as a harlot, but she owned and operated an Inn or Tavern. Being an Innkeeper suggests to us that she was an astute business woman, as well as, having multiple streams of income. She was prosperous by selling flax; operating an Inn and no doubt by her occupation as a prostitute. She was able to hide the spies when they came to her because it was harvest season and her flax was drying upon the roof in preparation to take to market. The roof was the perfect hiding place for her to take the spies to find protection.

Let's look at Joshua 2:1-3

1.   Now Joshua the son of Nun sent out two men from Acacia Grove to spy secretly, saying, "Go, and view the land, especially Jericho." So they went, and came to the house of a harlot named Rahab, and lodged there.

2.   And it was told the king of Jericho, saying, "Behold, men have come here tonight from the children of Israel to search out the country."

3.   So the king of Jericho sent to Rahab, saying, "Bring out the men who have come to you, who have entered your house, for they have come to search out all the country."

Rahab had the only Inn in town so male strangers were often seen entering and leaving her establishment. Also noted in historical accounts were visitors who came to the town of Jericho to go to Rahab's Inn, to seek information about the town's activity and the town's business. The Inn today would be similar to a Visitors Center only with lodging accommodations. You can now imagine why it was easy for the spies to seek her out without being detected.

Rahab engages in conversation with the spies about their intentions in her city she says in Joshua 2 9-11 *"I know that the Lord has given you the land, that the terror of you has fallen on us, and that all the inhabitants of the land are fainthearted because of you."*

For we have heard how the Lord dried up the water of the Red Sea for you when you came out of Egypt, and what you did to the two kings of the Amorites who were on the other side of the Jordan, Sihon and Og, whom you utterly destroyed.

And as soon as we heard these things, our hearts melted; neither did there remain any more courage in anyone because of you, for the Lord your God, He is God in heaven above and on earth beneath.

She is verifying to what she has heard about the children of Israel by prescribing how their God is an awesome and terrible God. She has a reverence for Joshua's God above that of her own god Ashtoreth. She continues to speak of Joshua's God as being mighty, having done great and awesome deeds among His people. He certainly had done mighty wonders in the land of their captivity and most recently delivered them from Egypt by parting the Red Sea.

107

No doubt, that in this time, this was a HUGE event and her engagement with the spies only solidified in her mind that she wanted to become a part of this great people. Her faith no doubt was on display.

Note:

God is willing and will do great feats or supernatural events on our behalf, in order to put fear or get the attention of our enemies. Remember in our story about the harlot from the City of Nain. This story is in Luke 7:11-16, ***Fear came upon all who witnessed the miracle of the widow's son being raised from the dead.*** The fear Luke is talking about was a fear that terrified them; they were afraid of what other things Jesus could do. They had never witnesses in this city a dead person coming back to life with a spoken word. Oh, I tell you a truth, when the enemy comes in like a flood; God raises his standard against the enemy. Fear had gripped the hearts of this people. God can be retaliatory toward His enemies. He has purposes to destroy those who try to destroy His people. The Old Testament is full of stories of how He set up ambushes against the children of Israel's enemies to destroy them, plunder them, and take the spoil! Hallelujah! Will He do that for us? Most certainly!

I like what David speaks in *Psalm 86:17, he says:* **Show me a sign for good, that those who hate me may see it and be ashamed, Because You Lord have helped me and comforted me.** We can make this same request of God on our behalf. We can make this our prayer when faced with challenging circumstances that the enemy has created.

Joshua 2:12-13

12. **Now therefore, I beg you, swear to me by the Lord, since I have shown you kindness, that you also will show kindness to my father's house, and give me a true token,**

13. **and spare my father, my mother, my brothers, my sisters, and all that they have, and deliver our lives from death."**

14. **So the men answered her, "Our lives for yours, if none of you tell this business of ours. And it shall be, when the Lord has given us the land that we will deal kindly and truly with you."**

Rahab is a negotiator. She has awesome skills and besides being very intelligent, she is perceptive, discerning, well informed, well connected within her community, and cares about her family. Her family is important to her. She is intrigued by the God of Israel, and is looking for the spies' protection when the City of Jericho is destroyed. She is unafraid of coming into an agreement with the spies for the protection and well-being of all her household. She wants a great future for her and her family and wants to become a part of the people whose God is awesome and mighty, who will protect His children, as she wants to protect her family.

It is also noteworthy that her Inn, which was also her living quarters, was part of the Jericho wall. The children of Israel had marched around that wall for seven days, shouting and praising God but when the wall came down; history tells us that her house was still standing because of God's protection and preservation. She is destined to have a glorious future. Rahab was redeemed by promise and destined for purpose.

The whole city is in ruins but her house is still standing because of the "red scarlet cord "outside of her window. This red scarlet cord symbolizes the "blood" which was put on the outside of the children of Israel's doorpost when they were about to depart Egypt, the land of their bondage, signifying the blood covenant. This is a true testament to Psalms 91:7-8. *The scripture states; a thousand may fall at your side, and ten thousand at your right hand; but it shall not come near you. Only with your eyes shall you look and see the reward of the wicked.*

God wants us to know that He punishes the wicked when the wicked tries to punish us. God is Jehovah Gibbor, teaching our hands to war and our fingers to fight. He is Our Kinsman Redeemer, redeeming our lives from destruction, our Bulwark and Shield, our defender and protector, and the Righteous Judge, Jehovah Shaphat, passing judgement on our enemies.

What we learn from Rahab is that despite her past, God redeems this harlot and makes her a heroine! She is mentioned in the book of Hebrews Hall of Fame. Hebrews 11:30, 31.

Rahab does not lose her HOPE, Romans 5:5. Her HOPE had no shame and did not disappoint her.

In Hebrews 10:35, she did not cast away her confidence; she did not lose HOPE.

Romans 4:17 against all HOPE she believes the words spoken regarding the children of Israel and the promise of the spies to provide safety.

After Rahab was saved by the spies, she married Salmon who was a prince from the tribe of Judah. A new covenant is established making her old covenant with the world and sin null and void. This was symbolic of the Old Covenant and the New Covenant. Jesus was the surety for the New Covenant; making the New Covenant better than the old. Much like when The Lord comes into our life. Our life becomes new and the old life is done away with. Our old life might have had history that we are ashamed of but our new life has promise of better things to come. The stain of our sin will not keep us from our inheritance.

Rahab becomes the mother of Boaz, a faithful man of God, who marries Ruth who bears a son named Obed who would be the father of Jesse, the father of David whose lineage Jesus, the Messiah is born. She is made a respectable woman!

Rahab's transformation and acceptance into the family of God should give us Hope regarding our past mistakes. The heart of God is to translate us from the powers of darkness and bring us into His kingdom bestowing upon us His power and authority. Satan was stripped of power, brought to an open shame and cannot operate unless we give him back our power. We must understand and learn the language and privileges of God's kingdom. We have been given a commission that came with power. God is always looking for faith to be on display. He wants to see some evidence of faith, even though we may still have sin in our life if we execute our faith like Rahab, He will respond. God will not always strive with us so we must acknowledge our weaknesses and repent of our sins. He washes us with his blood, and gives us a promise and looks at us just as though we have not sinned.

Psalms 103: 9-13 says this, **The LORD is merciful and gracious, slow to anger, and plenteous in mercy.**
9. He will not always chide, neither will he keep his anger forever.
10. He hath not dealt with us after our sins; nor rewarded us according to our iniquities.
11. For as the heaven is high above the earth, so great is his mercy toward them that fear him.
12. As far as the east is from the west, so far hath he removed our transgressions from us.
13. Like as a father pitieth his children, so the LORD pitieth them that fear him.

Yes, there are times when we are struggling to walk in purity but know today God does not punish us and use our circumstances against us. God will not hold us hostage to our sin. Yes, we live in the dispensation of Grace, but we do not have a license to keep on sinning. He reveals His truth to us and we acknowledge that truth, embrace the truth and that truth will set us free. The truth of God's word then becomes our daily guide and we live a repentant life. Do not buy the lies of Satan; *if we confess our sins God forgives us.* I John 1:9.

I loved this scene in the movie when Mr. Lewis is taking Vivian into the hotel where he has taken residence in the Penthouse Suite. The room is plush, ritzy and the epitome of wealth and luxury. He looks at the way Vivian is dressed. She is dressed like a "lady of the evening," with her very short skirt and revealing halter type top, and long leg high heel boots. You get the picture, he realizes that he needs to cover her up. He takes off his coat and wraps it around her before they enter the hotel lobby and make their way up to the penthouse suite.

This reminds me so much of what the Father does for us on our way to the Penthouse of our Promise Land. On the way to the Penthouse of our Purpose, He takes His mantle and covers our imperfections, He covers our iniquities, He covers our transgressions against Him, and He covers our weaknesses. The Love covers a multitude of sin, according to Proverbs 10:12.

Rahab: A Type of the Gentile Church

Rahab's status changed from a harlot to a heroine, from a gentile without a covenant, to a believer with a new covenant. She was a common harlot but was transformed to a great woman of faith, *a pretty woman*, and a woman of courage as mentioned in Hebrews 11:31, which states, ***by faith the*** *harlot Rahab did not perish with those who did not believe, when she had received the spies with peace.* Again, in James 3:25, *which says likewise, was not Rahab the harlot also justified by works when she received the messengers and sent them* **away.**

It is interesting to me that Paul, the author of the book of Hebrews; and James's Epistle refer to Rahab as the "harlot." Both Paul and James saw and mentioned her past life, and her old nature. Paul and James were inspired of the Holy Spirit to mention her acts or deeds of faith for future generations to glean and focus on her future. Satan and others might remember our past or old lifestyles of sin but God has redeemed us so that we are new creations in Christ; old things have passed away; behold all things have become new according to I Corinthians 5:17. If Hebrews 11:6 is correctly translated, we see that *"without faith it is impossible to please Him, for he who comes to God must believe that He is and that He rewards those who diligently seek Him."*

Rahab not only believed in what she heard about Joshua and the children of Israel, she believed in Joshua's God. God therefore rewards her faith by including her in the bloodline of Jesus. Rahab's marriage to Salmon who was a very prominent man within the nation of Judah and who by historical accounts referred to as a Prince. Rahab having married into royalty is now a legitimate Princess. "Rahab" is a "pretty women," a princess, having left her past of idolatry and harlotry in exchange for royalty. *"We are betrothed to God and He considers us as His chosen; His royal; His holy and special people that we may proclaim the praises of Him who called us out of darkness into His marvelous light,* according to 1 Peter 2:9.

Scholars believe Rahab served as a symbolic foreshadowing of the church and Gentile believer having become the first Gentile convert that was recorded in the Bible. She left her pagan beliefs in exchange for a relationship with the covenant keeping El Elohe Yisrael, The God of Israel.

Rahab, even though an idolatrous harlot, had faith growing based upon what she heard about the children of Israel. A seed was planted in her hearing that she continued to long for more. The more she heard of the conquest of the children of Israel, the more she wanted to become a part of their nation. Our faith comes much the same way, *by hearing, and hearing the Word of God.* (Romans 10:17). All of us have been given a measure of faith that has the potential for growth. Jesus reminded the disciples that their faith would increase to be able to do greater works than He wrought.

Faith is a required element to living in the kingdom, of God. We see evidences of faith in the Old Testament as well as in the New Testament. Faith is a Kingdom principle that God expects us as believers to live by, and expects us to develop in faith. Rahab's faith caused her to take a risk in negotiating with Joshua's spies. Her faith was rewarded and her whole household was delivered from death and destruction.

In the beginning Adam and Eve were God's family living an extraordinary life in the Garden of Eden, and enjoying intimate fellowship with their Father and Creator every day. When they yielded to disobedience, and failed their Father, God the Creator declared to Satan that his family would be redeemed, reconciled, and restored. By covering their nakedness with animal skin, their Father symbolically covered them with the shedding of blood. Likewise, the scarlet thread outside of Rahab's window symbolically represented the blood of Jesus, which would be shed to deliver His people and His family. The scarlet dye used in the fabric was imported from Egypt and could not be easily washed out and therefore rending permanent and enduring.

Our covenant with God is a lasting and enduring covenant that He keeps from one generation to the next. Historically, the color scarlet was also embroidered into the ephod, breastplate, and girdle of the high priest. The ephod looked like a tunic covering, and was placed upon the chest; much like God putting us in His heart and Jesus, our High Priest, making intercession for us according to Hebrews 7: 24, 25. God wanted His word written and embedded on the tablets of our hearts, forever reminding us of our relationship and proximity to Him. The robe placed upon Jesus to mock Him as **"the King of the Jews",** was a scarlet robe. In other words, symbolically, the Man Jesus, the man born with a flesh and bone body was covered with his own blood. In the realm of spiritual warfare, we are to pray and cover ourselves or apply the blood over all that we want protected from premature death and destruction from Satan and demonic activity. Exodus 12:13 *says* ***Now the blood shall be a sign for you on the houses where you are. When I see the blood, I will pass over you and the plague shall not be on you to destroy you when I strike the land.*** First Peter 2: 5 says ***we are being built up us as a spiritual house, a holy priesthood to offer up sacrifices acceptable to God through Jesus Christ.*** God marked those that are His and those He wants preserved and protected, see Genesis 4:15;

Psalm 37:37; Psalms 48:13; Ezekiel 9:4-6. Just as God marked what belongs to Him, Satan marks those that belong to him that worship him. See Revelations 13:17; Revelations 14:9, 11; Revelations 16:2; and Revelations 19:20.

Satan understands the power of blood covering, and he is rendered powerless when he sees it. On the night of the Passover meal, when the angel of death came to claim the lives of the Egyptians firstborn children, death had to pass over those houses with the blood on the doorpost. We too can appropriate the blood covering to stay the hand of our enemy.

Chapter Six:

Redeemed by Promise

Hosea 3:1-5, **The Lord said to me, Go again, love a woman who is loved by a lover and is committing adultery, just like the love of the Lord for the children of Israel who look to other gods and love the raisin cakes of the pagans. So I bought her for myself for fifteen shekels of silver and one and one half homers of barley. And I said to her, you shall stay with me many days, you shall not play the harlot, nor shall you have a man- so too, will I be toward you. For the children of Israel shall abide many days without king or prince without sacrifice or sacred pillar, without ephod or teraphim. Afterward, they shall return and seek the Lord their God and David shall be their king. They shall fear the Lord and His goodness in the latter days.**

I love this part of the story. It so displays Gods tenderness and loyalty to His covenant word and His unwavering love for His people, His family; you and me. In other words, God is going to make the ultimate purchase for Himself. He is foretelling His plan of redemption. Hosea's story is symbolically likened unto the behavior of God's people and despite the double mindedness and disobedience of His people, God wants them back. He wants you and me back regardless of the cost; regardless of our lifestyle; regardless of our having played the harlot.

The children of Israel had ephods and teraphims in their houses for worship. The ephod mentioned here was an image of Jehovah, which was overlaid with gold, or silver, it was not a part of the high priest ceremonial garments when making atonement on behalf of the people. The teraphim were idols in the form of human shapes; large and small reminiscent of ancestors which were respected by the Romans but were reverenced by the Hebrews, apparently household gods that were known to give prosperity to those who worshiped them. Michal, David's first wife is said to have prepared one of these teraphim gods and put it into a bed. She put a cap made from goat's hair on it that was typically worn by "sleepers and invalids." Today we would call this a stocking cap; she then covered the teraphim with a mantle or coverlet.

When Saul's soldiers came looking for David, she pointed to the teraphim and said that he was confined to his bed because of illness (1 Samuel 19:13-16). This trickery allowed David time to escape from Saul's soldiers. Saul who through his rebellion and disobedience to God; was influenced by the ruling principality of Jezebel and Athaliah. He became oppressed by their ruling demonic activity of lying, confusion, depression, witchcraft and a murderous spirit. He too, resorted to using teraphims and ultimately lost his reign as Israel's king and it cost him the lives of his sons, Jonathan, Abinadab, and Malchishua. (1 Samuel 31:2)

Verse 5: God declares that His children, *the children of Israel shall return and seek the Lord their God and David their King, in the latter days.* This is the revelation of His divine plan of redemption and foretelling of Israel's Savior to be manifested through David's bloodline.

I want to get personal here because I am talking about the spirit of harlotry. This spirit takes us away from having a true intimate relationship with the Father. God the Father longs for the hearts of His people to be restored to Him. He longs to have intimate fellowship with you and me; the **"Pretty Women"** in His life who totally lean and depends on Him to make us feel secure while He lavishes us with all of who He is because of our adoration and worship to Him.

After the divorce, I secured a good job as a department manager for a retail department store and I was doing well financially. I immersed myself totally into this career and a year later received a big promotion as an area manager for their upscale flagship store. The only thing missing from this time of success in my life was a man. I still had a desperate need to be in a relationship that brought me comfort, security, and affection. I still suffered from rejection and abandonment and needed to be wanted by someone, anyone. I had not yet conquered the physical desires that were easily aroused whenever I felt alone, or when I heard a song or remembered what it was like to be married. When I left work, I had to deal with the harsh reality that I went home to an empty house and an empty bed.

One weekend I was invited to a party, and met someone with whom I found to be good looking; tender and made me feel secure. At the beginning of the relationship, it was cordial and safe. He was respectful and said he understood my desire not to have sex outside of marriage. As the relationship ensued, so did the advances and I could no longer resist his aggressions to become sexually active. Much like Delilah's seductive enticements, I too became weak and fell prey to his advances. I became intoxicated with his tenderly holding me, and his gentle kisses. Satan is just like this, he is so subtle at first, making us feel comfortable and safe, then he becomes aggressive. I could not believe the first time we made love how disappointed I was to find out that this man was impotent. I was in a relationship with a man who was impotent. Yes, he was impotent! The outside of the package was just what I thought I wanted and needed and even though this relationship was frustrating I could not break away from the need I had for physical intimacy that I so desperately needed.

Just recently, I heard God describe that relationship to me "as one that was hot and heavy in foreplay but failed to satisfy the deep longings of my inner most being." I was trying to satisfy a spiritual need with a carnal remedy by returning to playing the harlot. I stayed in the relationship hoping each time it would get better but it never did.

A year or two before my divorce I had accepted the call to teach and preach the gospel and I received my license to do so. Now, after the divorce I am a backslidden minister having forsaken that calling. My passion for God and things that were important to Him were no longer important to me and were gone. I made little time to be in regular fellowship with other believers. I felt unclean and that everyone that looked at me could see right through me. Even though I was miserable, I did not care. Even though I was frustrated with my circumstances, I did nothing about them. I was terribly wounded by the pain of losing a marriage, losing my son in the custody battle and now being sexually impure. I felt my life had no credibility because of all the damaging evidence brought on by the stain of divorce.

The plan of Satan to derail my purpose, and abort the ministry call on my life was at work. However, God was about to hedge me in, just like Hosea was told to do with Gomer, the harlot in *Hosea 2:6, 7* **which says, I will hedge up your way with thorns and I will wall her in, so that she cannot find her path. She will chase her lovers, but not overtake them. Yes, she will chase or seek her lovers but will not find them, and she will return to her Husband.**

In the spring of 1991, I had a disastrous inventory on my job. I was told I was not being fired, but I was being demoted. I was humiliated and embarrassed. I thought I had done everything right to secure the right outcome. I was at the pinnacle of my career and the height of success. In previous inventories I had been acknowledged for my successes but now again, I found myself at the bottom of a very dark time in my life. I reached out to my best friend and she invited me to a conference in Houston she was hosting. It was there that I received a prophetic word in the ladies bathroom, from the keynote speaker. She told me that the Lord nudged her to come into the bathroom and she took my hands in a clasp, looked deeply into my eyes and said, "Your restoration is here in Houston."

Well; to make a long story short. It took me only three days to move from Dallas and return to Houston to begin a new journey with the Lord and to get away from this destructive relationship. I gave away most of all that I had knowing I did not want to bring anything from my past to my new future. Although I had lost everything, I was gaining something much more precious in my relationship with the Lord, my new Lover, Jehovah Kanna.

In August 1993, I was at my office working late, when I was dealt another blow. I received a phone call from the police to inform me that my daughter was found dead in her apartment and they had reason to believe she committed suicide. Hanging up the phone, I screamed to God, "you told me that my restoration was here in Houston and this is not restoration." I could not grasp what was happening; I was trying to understand God's idea of restoration. Getting on the plane the following day to bury my child, I found myself reliving some of the loss I had experienced. One thing was certain; I had become grounded and rooted in the word. I was on firm footing in my relationship with the Lord so I could weather this storm. I could trust my Father God who brought great comfort and peace like the one I had not known before.

In the months prior to my daughter's death, she had begun trying to reconcile our relationship and asked me to forgive her for the turbulent rebellious years of her life. I could not make any sense of her decision to end her life. However, the Lord gave me a word from Isaiah 57:1-2, which says, ***"the righteous perishes, and no man takes it to heart. Merciful men are taken away, while no one considers that the righteous is taken away from evil, he shall enter into peace, they shall rest in their beds, each one walking in his uprightness."*** Her death was untimely, but the Lord assured me she was with Him. My daughter was protected from the temptations that might have overpowered her and He knew I would be all right. His word had nourished me back to life, and His word would give me Hope.

Like Gomer, He beckoned me to come; He brought me into the wilderness and spoke comfort to me. He gave me vineyards from there; and the Valley of Achor as a door of hope. My door of Hope was indeed in Houston. God made a way of escape for me from the temptation that was designed to destroy my future.

And it shall be, in that day, says the Lord That you will call me My Husband and no longer call Me My Master. He was being my husband. For, I will take from

your mouth the names of Baals. They shall be remembered by their names no more. My lips were filled with praise and worship for Him. In that day, I will make a covenant for them. They will lie down in safety. I found safety in being in His presence. He had become my strong tower, Jehovah Migdal (Proverbs 18:10). I will betroth you to Me forever, Yes I will betroth you to Me in righteousness and justice; in loving kindness and mercy. I will betroth you in faithfulness. Then I shall say to those who were not my people, you are my people! And they shall say you are My God!

Hosea's marriage to the harlot Gomer portrays God's marriage to His harlot, the children of Israel, as well as His children of today. We play the harlot by giving our attention to jobs, careers, relationships, money, and other things. When our affection for these things is greater than our affection for God, we ignore our lover Jehovah Kanna, our Lord becomes very jealous. It is so important to know that the price He paid for us to ransom us back from the hands of Satan was His life. The Bible tells us that there is no greater Love than a man lay down his life. Jehovah Kanna did just that.

Pretty Woman

Chapter Seven:

Destined for Purpose

Much like the movie, the harlot gets tired of playing the harlot. She remembered the taste of her strawberry and champagne moment. When they arrived at the penthouse Edward immediately ordered big luscious strawberries and champagne, and told her the champagne brought out the sweetness of the strawberry. The taste in her mouth had not left but lingered as she remembered the sweet and satisfying goodness of someone she came to love. I guess David felt much the same way when he penned Psalm 34:8, *Oh taste and see that the Lord is good!*

Vivian had been transformed not only on the outside but also on the inside. She discovered the hidden person within herself who had greater potential. She knows, oh yes, she is certain that she wants more. Edward, can't come to terms that he no longer possesses the one thing he tried to purchase but is no longer in possession of it. He too realizes he wants more and decides he must go after what he has always been looking for.

The last scene shows Edward riding in a limousine with a contemplative look. He stops the car, jumps out to buy some roses; an operatic song fills the air while he is standing up through the sunroof, with his arms outstretched shouting "Princess Vivian, Princess Vivian."

Oh, my God this is so much like how the Father calls us by name and repeatedly chases after us. My thoughts went to Calvary. His arms were outstretched and nailed to the Cross; Christ wore a crown of thorns upon His head. For a moment I could hear him calling my name, tears were streaming down my face as I thanked Him for loving me "to death." **Pretty Women**, He is reminding us that we are His Bride; He comes running after us, regardless of the life, that we have lived estranged from Him. He shouts for the entire world to hear, to see and know that He wants us more than we could ever realize. Yes, He wants to betroth us to Him in Holy Matrimony! He whispers in our hearing He has come to deliver us, to take us away from the past of our lives and unite us to our future.

God's covenant name, Jehovah Kanna denotes the profound intense passion with which God wants to be enthralled. He want us to be captivated by Him, preoccupied with Him, enraptured by His presence, absorbed by who He is! Totally saturated by all He represents in Deity and Sovereignty. He does not want us to make room in our hearts for anyone but Him. When we have pledged our love, our loyalty, and allegiance to Him through intimate relationship, then and only then does He allow us to have the promise of relationship with others.

I remember well the command for Abraham to offer up Isaac. This was the promise seed. God had to know where in position He was compared to Isaac. God found it necessary to test Abraham's "heart of affection." It was more than just a sacrifice; it was a revelation of what was lodged deeply in the heart of Abraham. Would he choose God or would he choose the promise that took 25 years to manifest. God said, "Now I know what is in your heart, because you are willing to give me your son." Get that. God said, "He now knows. God the Sovereign God, now knows."

God will and must test our "heart of affection." We must come to know to whom we will sell our soul. We must be fully persuaded that all we need and want is God-Jehovah Kanna. When that is no longer an issue in our relationship with Him, He will give us what He desires for us. **Psalm 37:4 states: *Delight yourself also in the Lord and He shall give you the desires of our heart.***

I like the Complete Jewish Bible translation, which says; ***Then, you will delight yourself also in Adonai and He will give you your heart's desire.*** Conveying to me in a most intimate way, just how much ecstasy, and pleasure is exchanged from me to my Lord and from my Lord to me. An exchange that brings about conception of something very special and endearing that one can hardly wait until her time of delivery. Only the depth of His Love can capture that moment so perfectly.

There are times in our journey, along the road to our destiny, along the road to success, while climbing the corporate ladder or while in the wilderness without a sign of the promise that we play the Harlot. But, we don't have to! Don't be afraid of heights like Edward which was a natural fear. He was afraid of going to a higher elevation in his old relationships, which I saw as a spiritual fear. Then he met Vivian and he had to take a risk by looking up! That risk caused him to go where he had never gone before; and experience what he had been longing for. He had to take a risk. He had to Look Up. Remember, You are **that** *Pretty Woman......*

Sources Consulted

1. Freed Sandie, Breaking the Threefold Demonic Cord Chosen Books, Grand Rapids, Michigan, 2008

2. M.G. Easton MA D.D. Illustrated Bible Dictionary, Third Edition, Thomas Nelson, 1897

3. The Complete Jewish Bible by David H. Stern. Copyright © 1998. All rights reserved. Used by permission of Messianic Jewish Publishers, 6120 Day Long Lane, Clarksville, MD 21029. www.messianicjewish.net.

4. Dake, Finnis Jennings, Annotated Reference Bible, Dake Publishing Company, Lawrenceville, GAQ, 2015

Pretty Woman

About the Author:
Joanne M. Green

Intrigued with the world of fashion, Joanne became a runway model for the exclusive Lord and Taylor brand in New York and Boston. While enjoying her modeling success, her college studies reflected that interest and she received a Bachelor of Arts Degree in Fashion Merchandising. While managing her home life as a wife, mother and budding designer living in Dallas Texas, she embarked upon her entrepreneurial skills and launched "Ezra "a unique custom clothing line designed for women and children. Joanne sold her fashions to boutiques and marketed at trade and trunk shows. Joanne quickly discovered that her work was thrusting her into the brokenness and spiritually bankrupt lives of professionals from corporate backgrounds and lifestyles. Her work evolved from designing for the outward individual to ministering to the inward and thus sharing the word of God became an ensuing passion.

In 1981, she acknowledged and prepared for the prophetic call on her life by attending Word of Faith Bible School. She was licensed to preach and teach in 1984 by her Pastor, Ron Shaw, Dallas Texas, and ordained 1994 by

Bishop D. W. Washington, Houston, Texas, where she also served as an Associate Pastor for more than twenty years. Her professional experience has included Sales and Marketing Management, as well as Human Resource Management. She is an Executive Board Member of L.I.F.E. Inc., and is currently serving as an Executive Board Member, True Vineyard Ministries, San Marcos, Texas. This non-profit organization meets fundamental needs and provides sustainable income projects to widows affected with HIV/AIDS living in Rwanda, Africa.

Joanne believes that in the multitude of counselors, there is safety and spiritual covering. She has been mentored by the following: Bishop Dorothy Washington, Houston, Texas, Apostle Jerome and Pastor Betty Nelson, Houston, Texas, and Bishop Ernestine Reems, Oakland, California.

Her community involvement included serving as a juvenile volunteer in the Fairfield, California Correctional System; Religious Program Coordinator, Galveston Texas Prison Medical Facility; and Fort Bend Women's Center for Battered and Abused Women, where she currently offers Inner Healing classes. She has traveled domestically and globally sharing the Word of God, volunteering and serving in mission outreaches. In 2005, "Ezra" became Ezra Ministries, taken from the scripture found in Ezra 7:10. In

2014, Ezra Ministries was incorporated as a non-profit organization. Joanne has been called to be a modern day Ezra with the mandate to influence lives through her gifting to preach the uncompromised truth, teach the word simply, and to motivate people to become passionate and purposeful about kingdom principles.

Contact Information:
Ezra Ministries, Inc.
102 Wonder World Drive, Suite 304-126
San Marcos, Texas, 78666
Office- 512-270-9059
www.ezraministriesinc.org

Made in the USA
Coppell, TX
12 April 2022